Frommer's® PORTABLE Cancún

3rd Edition

by David Baird & Lynne Bairstow

Here's what critics say about Frommer's:

"Amazingly easy to use. Very portable, very complete."

—*Booklist*

"Detailed, accurate, and easy-to-read information for all price ranges."

—*Glamour Magazine*

"Hotel information is close to encyclopedic."

—*Des Moines Sunday Register*

"Frommer's Guides have a way of giving you a real feel for a place."

—*Knight Ridder Newspapers*

WILEY

Wiley Publishing, Inc.

Published by:

WILEY PUBLISHING, INC.
111 River St.
Hoboken, NJ 07030-5774

ISBN-13: 978-0-7645-8898-3
ISBN-10: 0-7645-8898-2

Editor: Margot Weiss
Production Editor: Heather Wilcox
Cartographer: Andrew Murphy
Photo Editor: Richard Fox
Production by Wiley Indianapolis Composition Services

Front cover photo: Snorkelers feeding fish.

For information on our other products and services or to obtain technical support, please contact our Customer Care Department within the U.S. at 800/762-2974, outside the U.S. at 317/572-3993 or fax 317/572-4002.

Wiley also publishes its books in a variety of electronic formats. Some content that appears in print may not be available in electronic formats.

Manufactured in the United States of America

5 4 3 2 1

Contents

List of Maps

About the Authors

David Baird has lived in various parts of Latin America, including Mexico, Puerto Rico, Peru, and Brazil. He now makes his home in Austin, Texas, but he tries to get back to the turquoise-blue waters of the Yucatán whenever possible because he thinks he looks good in that color.

For **Lynne Bairstow,** Mexico has become more home than her native United States. For most of the past 13 years, she has lived in Puerto Vallarta, where she has developed a true appreciation and respect for the customs, culture, and natural treasures of Mexico. Her travel articles on Mexico have appeared in the *New York Times, Los Angeles Times, Private Air* magazine, *Luxury Living* magazine, and the in-flight magazines of Mexicana Airlines and Alaska Airlines. In 2000, Lynne was awarded the Pluma de Plata, a top honor granted by the Mexican government to foreign writers, for her work in the Frommer's guidebook to Puerto Vallarta.

Acknowledgments

David Baird would like to acknowledge an enormous debt to Ms. Claudia Hurtado, whose knowledge and contacts in the Riviera Maya smoothed the way for his research of that area. He would also like to extend a personal thanks to all the readers who have taken the time to write him with their suggestions.

Lynne Bairstow is appreciative of the invaluable contribution of her research assistant, Alejandra Macedo, to her work on this book.

An Invitation to the Reader

In researching this book, we discovered many wonderful places—hotels, restaurants, shops, and more. We're sure you'll find others. Please tell us about them, so we can share the information with your fellow travelers in upcoming editions. If you were disappointed with a recommendation, we'd love to know that, too. Please write to:

Frommer's Portable Cancún, 3rd Edition
Wiley Publishing, Inc. • 111 River St. • Hoboken, NJ 07030-5774

An Additional Note

Please be advised that travel information is subject to change at any time—and this is especially true of prices. We therefore suggest that you write or call ahead for confirmation when making your travel plans. The authors, editors, and publisher cannot be held responsible for the experiences of readers while traveling. Your safety is important to us, however, so we encourage you to stay alert and be aware of your surroundings. Keep a close eye on cameras, purses, and wallets, all favorite targets of thieves and pickpockets.

Frommer's Star Ratings, Icons & Abbreviations

Every hotel, restaurant, and attraction listing in this guide has been ranked for quality, value, service, amenities, and special features using a **star-rating system.** In country, state, and regional guides, we also rate towns and regions to help you narrow down your choices and budget your time accordingly. Hotels and restaurants are rated on a scale of zero (recommended) to three stars (exceptional). Attractions, shopping, nightlife, towns, and regions are rated according to the following scale: zero stars (recommended), one star (highly recommended), two stars (very highly recommended), and three stars (must-see).

In addition to the star-rating system, we also use **seven feature icons** that point you to the great deals, in-the-know advice, and unique experiences that separate travelers from tourists. Throughout the book, look for:

Finds	Special finds—those places only insiders know about
Fun Fact	Fun facts—details that make travelers more informed and their trips more fun
Kids	Best bets for kids—advice for the whole family
Moments	Special moments—those experiences that memories are made of
Overrated	Places or experiences not worth your time or money
Tips	Insider tips— great ways to save time and money
Value	Great values—where to get the best deals

The following **abbreviations** are used for credit cards:

AE	American Express	DISC	Discover	V	Visa
DC	Diners Club	MC	MasterCard		

FROMMERS.COM

Now that you have the guidebook to a great trip, visit our website at **www.frommers.com** for travel information on more than 3,000 destinations. With features updated regularly, we give you instant access to the most current trip-planning information available. At Frommers.com, you'll also find the best prices on airfares, accommodations, and car rentals—and you can even book travel online through our travel booking partners. At Frommers.com, you'll also find the following:

- Online updates to our most popular guidebooks
- Vacation sweepstakes and contest giveaways
- Newsletter highlighting the hottest travel trends
- Online travel message boards with featured travel discussions

1

Planning Your Trip to Cancún

A little planning can make the difference between a good trip and a great trip. When should you go? What's the best way to get there? How much should you plan on spending? What festivals or special events will be taking place during your visit? What safety or health precautions are advised? We'll answer these and other questions for you in this chapter. In addition to these basics, I highly recommend taking a little time to learn about the culture and traditions of Mexico. It can make the difference between simply getting away and adding true understanding to your experience.

THE REGION AT A GLANCE

Travelers to the Yucatán Peninsula will have an opportunity to see pre-Hispanic ruins—such as **Chichén Itzá, Cobá,** and **Tulum**—and the living descendants of the cultures that built them, as well as the ultimate in resort Mexico: **Cancún.** The peninsula borders the dull aquamarine Gulf of Mexico on the west and the north, and the clear blue Caribbean Sea on the east. It covers almost 217,560 square kilometers (84,000 sq. miles), with nearly 1,610km (1,000 miles) of shoreline. Underground rivers and natural wells called *cenotes* are a peculiar feature of this region.

Lovely rock-walled Maya villages and crumbling henequén haciendas dot the interior of the peninsula. And just 12.9km (8 miles) northeast of Cancún, a quick boat ride away, is **Isla Mujeres,** a small village peppered with shops, cafes, and tranquil beaches.

1 Visitor Information

SOURCES OF INFORMATION

The **Mexico Hotline** (✆ **800/44-MEXICO**) is an excellent source of general information; you can request brochures on the country and get answers to the most commonly asked questions.

Abundant information about Mexico is available on the Mexican Tourist Promotion Council's website, **www.visitmexico.com**.

The **U.S. State Department** (✆ **202/647-5225;** http://travel.state.gov) has a "Tips for Travelers to Mexico" information sheet,

Cancún & Environs

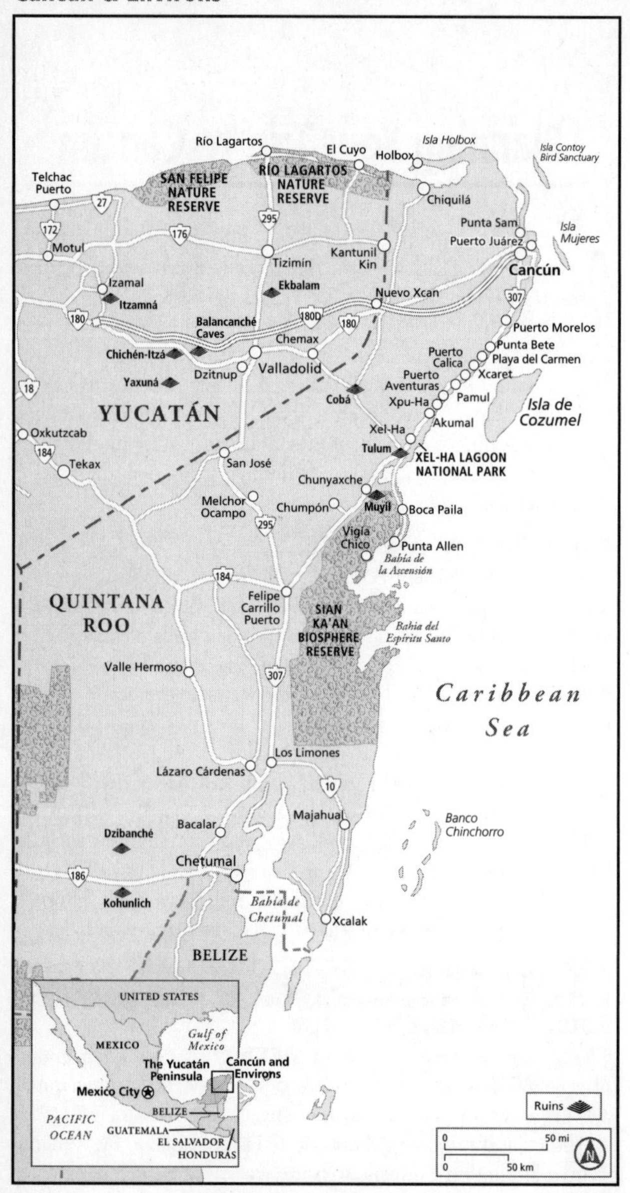

Destination Mexico: Red Alert Checklist

- Has the **U.S. State Department** (http://travel.state.gov) issued any travel advisories regarding Mexico? (Mexico is considered at low risk for a terrorist attack; few event schedule changes or building closings have been instituted.)
- Do you have your passport or official ID? If traveling in a coastal area, did you pack insect repellent? Sunblock? A hat? Sunglasses? A sweater or jacket?
- Do you need to book tour, restaurant, or travel reservations in advance?
- Did you make sure attractions and activities that interest you are operating? Some attractions, such as seasonal nature tours, sell out quickly.
- If you purchased traveler's checks, have you recorded the check numbers, and stored the documentation separately from the checks?
- Do you have your credit card personal identification numbers (PINs)?
- If you have an e-ticket, do you have documentation?
- Do you know the address and phone number of your country's embassy?

plus a **Consular Information Sheet** with safety, medical, driving, and general travel information gleaned from reports by official U.S. State Department offices in Mexico. You can also request the Consular Information Sheet by fax (202/647-3000).

The **Centers for Disease Control Hotline** (© **800/311-3435** or 404/639-3534; www.cdc.gov) is another source of medical information affecting travelers. The center's website provides information on health issues for specific countries. The CDC Travelers' Health toll-free hotline number is © **877/FYI-TRIP.** The toll-free fax number for requesting information is 888/232-3299, and any information available by fax is also available at **www.cdc.gov/travel**. There you'll also find links to health resources for people traveling with children or with special needs, as well as tips on safe food and water. The U.S. State Department offers medical information for Americans traveling abroad at **http://travel.state.gov**. This site provides general information and lists of doctor/hospitals abroad.

MEXICO TOURISM BOARD OFFICES In North America, the following offices offer tourism information:

United States: Chicago (✆ **312/606-9252**), Houston (✆ **713/772-2581,** ext. 105), Los Angeles (✆ **213/351-2069;** fax 213/351-2074), Miami (✆ **305/282-9112**), and New York (✆ **212/308-2110**). The Mexican Embassy is at 1911 Pennsylvania Ave. NW, Washington, DC 20005 (✆ **202/728-1750**).

Canada: 1 Place Ville-Marie, Suite 1931, Montréal, QUE, H3B 2C3 (✆ **514/871-1052**); 2 Bloor St. W., Suite 1502, Toronto, ON, M4W 3E2 (✆ **416/925-0704**); 999 W. Hastings, Suite 1110, Vancouver, BC, V6C 2W2 (✆ **604/669-2845**). Embassy office: 1500-45 O'Connor St., Ottawa, ON, K1P 1A4 (✆ **613/233-8988;** fax 613/235-9123).

2 Entry Requirements & Customs

ENTRY REQUIREMENTS

All travelers to Mexico are required to present **proof of citizenship,** such as an original birth certificate with a raised seal, a valid passport, or naturalization papers. Those using a birth certificate should also have current photo identification, such as a driver's license or official ID. If the last name on the birth certificate is different from your current name, bring a photo identification card *and* legal proof of the name change, such as the original marriage license or certificate. ***Note:*** Photocopies are *not* acceptable.

U.S. citizens reentering the U.S. must prove both citizenship *and* identification, so always carry a picture ID, such as a driver's license or a valid passport.

Please note that as of December 31, 2006, **a passport will be required** for all air and sea travel to and from Mexico.

You must carry a **Mexican Tourist Permit (FMT),** the equivalent of a tourist visa, which Mexican border officials issue, free of charge, after proof of citizenship is accepted. Airlines generally provide the necessary forms aboard your flight to Mexico. The FMT is more important than a passport in Mexico, so guard it carefully. If you lose it, you may not be permitted to leave the country until you can replace it—a bureaucratic hassle that can take anywhere from a few hours to a week.

The FMT can be issued for up to 180 days. Sometimes officials don't ask but just stamp a time limit, so be sure to say "6 months," or at least twice as long as you intend to stay. If you decide to extend your stay, you may request that additional time be added to your FMT from an official immigration office in Mexico.

Note: Children under age 18 traveling without parents or with only one parent must have a notarized letter from the absent parent(s) authorizing the travel.

CUSTOMS

When you enter Mexico, Customs officials will be tolerant as long as you have no illegal drugs or firearms. You're allowed to bring in two cartons of cigarettes or 50 cigars, plus a kilogram (2.2 lb.) of smoking tobacco; two 1-liter bottles of wine or hard liquor; and 12 rolls of film. A laptop computer, camera equipment, and sporting equipment (golf clubs, scuba gear, a bicycle) that could feasibly be used during your stay are also allowed. The underlying guideline is to not bring anything that looks as if it's meant to be resold in Mexico.

Returning **U.S. citizens** who have been away for at least 48 hours are allowed to bring back, once every 30 days, $800 worth of merchandise duty-free. You'll be charged a flat rate of 4% duty on the next $1,000 worth of purchases. Be sure to have your receipts handy. On mailed gifts, the duty-free limit is $200. Be sure to have your receipts or purchases handy to expedite the declaration process. ***Note:*** If you owe duty, you are required to pay on your arrival in the United States, either by cash, personal check, government or traveler's check, or money order, and in some locations, a Visa or MasterCard.

For a clear summary of **Canadian** rules, request the booklet *I Declare* from the **Canada Customs and Revenue Agency** (© **800/461-9999** in Canada, or 204/983-3500; www.ccra-adrc.gc.ca). Canada allows citizens a $750 exemption, and you're allowed to bring back duty-free one carton of cigarettes, 1 can of tobacco, 40 imperial ounces of liquor, and 50 cigars. In addition, you're allowed to mail gifts to Canada valued at less than $60 a day, provided they're unsolicited and don't contain alcohol or tobacco (write on the package "Unsolicited gift, under $60 value"). Declare all valuables on the Y-38 form before departure from Canada, including serial numbers of items you already own, such as expensive cameras. ***Note:*** The $750 exemption can only be used once a year and only after an absence of 7 days.

U.K. citizens returning from a non-E.U. country have a Customs allowance of: 200 cigarettes; 50 cigars; 250 grams of smoking tobacco; 2 liters of still table wine; 1 liter of spirits or strong liqueurs (over 22% volume); 2 liters of fortified wine, sparkling wine, or other liqueurs; 60cc (ml) of perfume; 250cc (ml) of toilet water; and £145 worth of all other goods, including gifts and souvenirs. People under 17 cannot have the tobacco or alcohol allowance. For more information, contact **HM Customs & Excise** (✆ **0845/010-9000,** or 020/8929-0152 from outside the U.K.; www.hmce.gov.uk).

The duty-free allowance in **Australia** is $400 or, for those under 18, $200. Citizens can bring in 250 cigarettes or 250 grams of loose tobacco, and 1,125ml of alcohol. If you're returning with valuables you already own, such as foreign-made cameras, file form B263. A helpful brochure, available from Australian consulates or Customs offices, is *Know Before You Go.* For more information, contact the **Australian Customs Services** (✆ **1300/363-263;** www.customs.gov.au).

The duty-free allowance for **New Zealand** is $700. Citizens over 17 can bring in 200 cigarettes, or 50 cigars, or 250 grams of tobacco (or a mixture if their combined weight doesn't exceed 250g); plus 4.5 liters of wine and beer, or 1.125 liters of liquor. New Zealand currency does not carry import or export restrictions. Fill out a certificate of export, listing the valuables you are taking out of the country; that way, you can bring them back without paying duty. A free pamphlet available at New Zealand consulates and Customs offices, *New*

Tips A Few Words about Prices

The peso's value continues to fluctuate—at press time, it was roughly 11 pesos to the dollar. Prices in this book (which are always given in U.S. dollars) have been converted to U.S. dollars at 11 pesos to the dollar. Most hotels in Mexico—with the exception of places that receive little foreign tourism—quote prices in U.S. dollars. Thus, currency fluctuations are unlikely to affect the prices charged by most hotels.

Mexico has a **value-added tax** of 15% (*Impuesto al Valor Agregado,* or IVA, pronounced "ee-bah") on almost everything, including restaurant meals, bus tickets, and souvenirs. An exception is Cancún, where the IVA is 10%; as a port of entry, it receives a break on taxes. Hotels charge the usual 15% IVA, plus a locally administered bed tax of 2% (in many but not all areas), for a total of 17%. In Cancún, hotels charge the 10% IVA plus 2% room tax. Prices quoted by hotels and restaurants will not necessarily include IVA. You may find that upper-end properties quote prices without IVA included, while lesser-price hotels include IVA. Always ask to see a printed price sheet, and always ask if the tax is included.

Money Matters

The **universal currency sign ($)** is used to indicate pesos in Mexico. The use of this symbol in this book, however, denotes U.S. currency.

Zealand Customs Guide for Travellers, Notice no. 4, answers most questions. For more information, contact **New Zealand Customs,** The Customhouse, 17–21 Whitmore St., Box 2218, Wellington (✆ **04/473-6099** or 0800/428-786; www.customs.govt.nz).

GOING THROUGH CUSTOMS Mexican Customs inspection has been streamlined. At most points of entry, tourists are requested to press a button in front of what looks like a traffic signal, which alternates on touch between red and green. With a green light, you go through without inspection; with a red light, your luggage or car may be inspected briefly or thoroughly. If you have an unusual amount of luggage or an oversized piece, you may be subject to inspection anyway.

3 Money

The currency in Mexico is the Mexican **peso.** Paper currency comes in denominations of 20, 50, 100, 200, 500, and 1,000 pesos. Coins come in denominations of 1, 2, 5, and 10 pesos, and 20 and 50 **centavos** (100 centavos equal 1 peso). The current exchange rate for the U.S. dollar is just less than 11 pesos; at that rate, an item that costs 11 pesos would be equivalent to US$1.

Getting **change** is a problem in Mexico. Small-denomination bills and coins are hard to come by, so start collecting them early in your trip and continue as you travel. Shopkeepers everywhere seem always to be out of change and small bills; that's doubly true in markets.

Many establishments that deal with tourists, especially in coastal resort areas, quote prices in dollars. To avoid confusion, they use the abbreviations "Dlls." for dollars and "M.N." (*moneda nacional,* or national currency) for pesos. All dollar equivalencies in this book were based on an exchange rate of 11 pesos per dollar.

The rate of exchange fluctuates a tiny bit daily, so you probably are better off not exchanging too much of your currency at once. Don't forget, however, to have enough pesos to carry you over a weekend or a Mexican holiday, when banks are closed. In general, avoid carrying the U.S. $100 bill, the bill most commonly counterfeited in Mexico and therefore the most difficult to exchange, especially in smaller towns. Small bills and coins in pesos are hard to come by in Mexico, so the U.S. $1 bill is very useful for tipping. ***Note:*** A tip in U.S. coins, which Mexican banks do not accept, is of no value to the service provider.

The bottom line on exchanging money of all kinds: It pays to ask first and shop around. Banks pay the top rates.

Exchange houses *(casas de cambio)* are generally more convenient than banks because they have more locations and longer hours; the rate of exchange may be the same as a bank's or only slightly lower. ***Note:*** Before leaving a bank or exchange-house window, always count your change in front of the teller before the next client steps up.

Large airports have currency-exchange counters that often stay open whenever flights are arriving or departing. Though convenient, these generally do not offer the most favorable rates.

A hotel's exchange desk commonly pays less favorable rates than banks; however, when the currency is in a state of flux, higher-priced hotels are known to beat bank rates, in an effort to attract dollars. It pays to shop around, but in almost all cases, you receive a better exchange by changing money first and then paying for goods or services, rather than by paying dollars directly to an establishment.

BANKS & ATMS Banks in Mexico are rapidly expanding and improving services. They tend to be open weekdays from 9am until 5pm, and often for at least a half-day on Saturday. In larger resorts and cities, they can generally accommodate the exchange of dollars (which used to stop at noon) anytime during business hours. During times when the currency is in flux, a particular bank may not exchange dollars, so check before standing in line. Don't even bother with personal checks drawn on a U.S. bank—the bank will wait for your check to clear, which can take weeks, before giving you your money.

The easiest and best way to get cash away from home is from an **ATM (automated teller machine).** Travelers to Mexico can easily withdraw money from ATMs in most major cities and resort areas. The U.S. State Department has an advisory against using ATMs in Mexico for safety reasons, stating that they should only be used during business hours, but this pertains primarily to Mexico City, where crime remains a significant problem. In most resorts in Mexico, the use of ATMs is perfectly safe—just use the same precautions you would at any ATM. The exchange rate is generally more favorable than that at a currency house. Most machines offer Spanish/English menus and dispense pesos, but some offer the option of withdrawing dollars. Universal bank cards, such as **Cirrus** (**© 800/424-7787**; www.mastercard.com) and **PLUS** (**© 800/843-7587**;

www.visa.com) can be used. Look at the back of your bank card to see which network you're on, then call or check online for ATM locations at your destination. Be sure your personal identification number (PIN) works in international destinations and find out your daily withdrawal limit before you leave home. Also keep in mind that many banks impose a fee every time a card is used at a different bank's ATM, and that fee can be higher for international transactions than for domestic ones.

You can also get cash advances on your credit card at an ATM. Keep in mind that credit card companies try to protect themselves from theft by limiting the funds someone can withdraw outside their home country, so call your credit card company before you leave home. And keep in mind that you'll pay interest from the moment of your withdrawal, even if you pay your monthly bills on time.

TRAVELER'S CHECKS Some, but not all, Mexican banks charge a service fee of about 1% to exchange traveler's checks. However, you can pay for most purchases directly with traveler's checks at the establishment's stated exchange rate. If you choose to carry traveler's checks, be sure to keep a record of their serial numbers separate from your checks in the event that they are stolen or lost. You'll get a refund faster if you know the numbers.

CREDIT CARDS Visa, MasterCard, and American Express are the most accepted cards. You'll be able to charge most hotel, restaurant, and store purchases, as well as almost all airline tickets, on your credit card. You generally can't charge gasoline purchases in Mexico. You can get cash advances of several hundred dollars on your card, but there may be a wait of 20 minutes to 2 hours.

Charges will be made in pesos, then converted into dollars by the bank issuing the credit card. Generally you receive the favorable

Tips **Dear Visa: I'm Off to Cancún!**

Some credit card companies recommend that you notify them of any impending trip abroad so that they don't become suspicious when the card is used numerous times in a foreign destination and block your charges. Even if you don't call your credit card company in advance, you can always use the card's toll-free emergency number (see "Lost & Stolen Property" under "Fast Facts," later in this chapter) if a charge is refused—a good reason to carry the phone number with you.

bank rate when paying by credit card. However, be aware that some establishments in Mexico add a 5% to 7% surcharge when you pay with a credit card. This is especially true when using American Express. Many times, advertised discounts will not apply if you pay with a credit card.

4 When to Go

High season begins around December 20 and continues through Easter. It is certainly the best time to be in the Yucatán if you're here for calm, warm weather; snorkeling, diving, and fishing (the calmer weather means clearer and more predictable seas); or if you plan to visit the ruins that dot the interior of the peninsula. Book well in advance if you plan to be in Cancún around the holidays.

Low season begins the day after Easter and continues to mid-December; during low season, prices may drop 20% to 50%. Increasingly in Cancún, demand by European visitors is creating a summer high season, with hotel rates approaching those charged in the winter months.

Generally speaking, Mexico's **dry season** runs from November to April, with the **rainy season** stretching from May to October. It isn't a problem if you're staying close to the beaches, but for those bent on road-tripping to Chichén Itzá or other sites, temperatures and humidity in the interior can be downright stifling from May to July. Later in the rainy season, the frequency of **tropical storms** and **hurricanes** increases. Storms can put a crimp in your vacation, but they can also cool off temperatures, making climbing ruins a real joy, accompanied by cool air and a slight wind. November is especially ideal for Yucatán travels. Cancún and Isla Mujeres also have a rainy season from November to January, when northern storms hit. Divers should be aware that this season is the least suitable for diving.

CANCÚN CALENDAR OF FESTIVALS & SPECIAL EVENTS

Note: All banks and official public offices in Mexico close on national holidays.

January

New Year's Day (Año Nuevo). National holiday. Parades, religious observances, parties, and fireworks welcome the New Year everywhere. In traditional indigenous communities, new tribal leaders are inaugurated with colorful ceremonies rooted in the pre-Hispanic past. January 1.

Three Kings Day (Día de Reyes). Nationwide. Commemorates the Three Kings bringing gifts to the Christ Child. On this day, children receive gifts, much like the traditional gift giving that accompanies Christmas in the United States. Friends and families gather to share the *Rosca de Reyes,* a special cake. Inside the cake is a small doll representing the Christ Child; whoever receives the doll in his or her piece must host a tamales-and-*atole* party the next month. January 6.

February

Candlemas (Día de la Candelaria). Nationwide. Music, dances, processions, food, and other festivities lead up to a blessing of seed and candles in a tradition that mixes pre-Hispanic and European traditions marking the end of winter. All those who attended the Three Kings Celebration reunite to share *atole* and tamales at a party hosted by the recipient of the doll found in the Rosca. February 2.

Constitution Day (Día de la Constitución). National holiday. Celebration in honor of the signing of the constitution that currently governs Mexico, signed in 1917 as a result of the revolutionary war of 1910. This holiday is celebrated with parades. February 5.

Carnaval. This celebration takes place the 3 days preceding Ash Wednesday and the beginning of Lent. It is celebrated with special gusto in Cozumel, where it resembles Mardi Gras in New Orleans, with a festive atmosphere and parades. Transportation and hotels are packed, so it's best to make reservations well in advance and arrive a couple of days before the beginning of celebrations. In 2006, the dates are February 26-28.

Ash Wednesday. The start of Lent and time of abstinence, this is a day of reverence nationwide, but some towns honor it with folk dancing and fairs. March 1 in 2006.

March–April

Benito Juárez's Birthday. National holiday. Small hometown celebrations crop up countrywide. March 21.

Spring Equinox, Chichén Itzá. On the first day of spring, the Temple of Kukulkán—Chichén Itzá's main pyramid—aligns with the sun, and the shadow of the plumed serpent moves slowly from the top of the building down. When the shadow reaches the bottom, the body joins the carved stone snake's head at the base of the pyramid. According to ancient legend, at the moment that the serpent is whole, the earth is fertilized to ensure a bountiful growing season. Visitors come from around the world to marvel at this sight, so advance arrangements are advisable. The shadow can be seen from March 19 to 23, but the best view is on March 21. Elsewhere, the equinox is celebrated with festivals and celebrations to welcome spring in the custom of the ancient Mexicans, with dances and prayers to the elements and the four cardinal points, to renew their energy for the year. It's customary to wear white with a red ribbon.

Holy Week. This celebrates the last week in the life of Christ from Palm Sunday to Easter Sunday with somber religious processions almost nightly, spoofing of Judas, and reenactments of specific biblical events, plus food and crafts fairs. Businesses close during this traditional week of Mexican national vacations.

If you plan on traveling to or around Mexico during Holy Week, make your reservations early. Airline seats on flights into and out of the country will be reserved months in advance. Buses to these towns or to almost anywhere in Mexico will be full, so try arriving on the Wednesday or Thursday before Good Friday. Easter Sunday is quiet, and the week following is a traditional vacation period.

May

Labor Day. National holiday. Workers' parades take place countrywide, and everything closes. May 1.

Holy Cross Day (Día de la Santa Cruz). Workers place a cross on top of unfinished buildings and celebrate with food, bands, folk dancing, and fireworks around the work site. May 3.

Cinco de Mayo. National holiday, Puebla and nationwide. This celebrates the defeat of the French at the Battle of Puebla. May 5.

Feast of San Isidro. The patron saint of farmers is honored with a blessing of seeds and work animals. May 15.

June

Navy Day (Día de la Marina). Celebrated in all coastal towns, with naval parades and fireworks. June 1.

Corpus Christi. Nationwide. The Body of Christ (the Eucharist) is honored with religious processions, Masses, and food. *Mulitas* (mules) handmade from dried cornhusks and painted (often with a corn-husk rider) and sometimes accompanied by pairs of corn-husk dolls are traditionally sold. Date varies.

Día de San Pedro (St. Peter and St. Paul's Day). Nationwide. Celebrated wherever St. Peter is the patron saint, this holiday honors anyone named Pedro or Peter. June 29.

August

Assumption of the Virgin Mary. Celebrated throughout the country with special Masses and, in some places, with processions. August 20 to August 22.

September

Independence Day. This day of parades, picnics, and family reunions throughout the country celebrates Mexico's independence from Spain. At 11pm on September 15, the president of Mexico gives the famous independence *grito* (shout) from the National Palace in Mexico City. At least half a million people are crowded into the *zócalo,* and the rest of the country watches the event on TV or participates in local celebrations, which mirror the festivities at the national level. An enormous military parade takes place on September 16. The schedule of events is exactly the same in every village, town, and city across Mexico. September 15 to September 16; September 16 is a national holiday.

Fall Equinox, Chichén Itzá. The same shadow play that occurs during the spring equinox repeats itself for the fall equinox. September 21 to September 22.

October

Día de la Raza ("Ethnicity Day" or Columbus Day). Commemorates the fusion of the Spanish and Mexican peoples. October 12.

November

Day of the Dead. What's commonly called the Day of the Dead is actually 2 days, All Saints' Day—honoring saints and deceased children—and All Souls' Day, honoring deceased adults. Relatives gather at cemeteries countrywide, carrying candles and food, and often spend the night beside the graves of loved ones. Weeks before, bakers begin producing bread formed in the shape of mummies or round loaves decorated with bread "bones." Decorated sugar skulls emblazoned with glittery names are sold everywhere. Many days ahead, homes and churches erect special altars laden with Day of the Dead bread, fruit, flowers, candles, favorite foods, and photographs of saints and of the deceased. On the 2 nights, children dress in costumes and masks, often carrying through the streets mock coffins and pumpkin lanterns, into which they expect money will be dropped. November 1 to November 2; November 1 is a national holiday.

Revolution Day. Commemorates the start of the Mexican revolution in 1910, with parades, speeches, rodeos, and patriotic events. November 20.

December

Feast of the Virgin of Guadalupe. Throughout the country, religious processions, street fairs, dancing, fireworks, and Masses honor the patroness of Mexico. This is one of Mexico's most moving and beautiful displays of traditional culture. The Virgin of Guadalupe appeared to a young man, Juan Diego, in December 1531, on a hill near Mexico City. He convinced the bishop that he had seen the apparition by revealing his cloak, upon which the Virgin was emblazoned. It's customary for children to dress up as Juan Diego, wearing mustaches and red bandanas. One of the most famous and elaborate celebrations takes place at the Basílica of Guadalupe, north of Mexico City, where the Virgin appeared. Every village celebrates this day, though, often with processions of children carrying banners of the Virgin and with *charreadas* (rodeos), bicycle races, dancing, and fireworks. December 12.

Christmas *Posadas*. On each of the 9 nights before Christmas, it's customary to reenact the Holy Family's search for an inn, with door-to-door candlelit processions in cities and villages nationwide. These are also hosted by most businesses and community organizations, taking the place of the northern tradition of a Christmas party. December 15 to December 24.

Christmas. Mexicans extend this celebration and often leave their jobs beginning 2 weeks before Christmas all the way through New Year's Day. Many businesses close, and resorts and hotels fill. Significant celebrations take place on December 23.

New Year's Eve. As in the rest of the world, New Year's Eve in Mexico is celebrated with parties, fireworks, and plenty of noise. December 31.

5 Travel Insurance

Check your existing insurance policies and credit-card coverage before you buy travel insurance. You may already be covered for canceled tickets, medical expenses, or lost luggage. The cost of travel insurance varies widely, depending on the cost and length of your trip, your age and health, and the type of trip you're taking.

The bottom line: Always, always check the fine print before you sign; more and more policies have built-in exclusions and restrictions that may leave you out in the cold if something goes awry.

Trip-cancellation insurance helps you get your money back if you have to back out of a trip, if you have to go home early, or if your travel supplier goes bankrupt. In this unstable world, trip-cancellation insurance is a good buy if you're getting tickets well in advance. Insurance policy details vary, so read the fine print—and especially make sure that your airline or cruise line is on the list of carriers covered in case of bankruptcy. For more information, contact one of the following recommended insurers: **Access America** (✆ 866/807-3982; www.accessamerica.com), **Travel Guard International** (✆ 800/826-4919; www.travelguard.com), **Travel Insured International** (✆ 800/243-3174; www.travelinsured.com), and **Travelex Insurance Services** (✆ 888/457-4602; www.travelex-insurance.com).

Most **health insurance** policies cover you if you get sick away from home—but check, particularly if you're insured by an HMO. With the exception of certain HMOs and Medicare/Medicaid, your medical insurance should cover medical treatment overseas. However, most hospitals make you pay your bills up front, and send you a refund after you've returned home and filed the necessary paperwork. If you require additional medical insurance, try **MEDEX International** (✆ 800/527-0218 or 410/453-6300; www.medexassist.com) or **Travel Assistance International** (✆ **800/821-2828;** www.travelassistance.com; for general information on services, call the company's Worldwide Assistance Services, Inc., ✆ **800/777-8710**).

On domestic flights, checked **baggage** is covered up to $2,500 per ticketed passenger. On international flights (including U.S. portions of international trips), baggage is limited to approximately $9.07 per pound, up to approximately $635 per checked bag. If you plan to check items more valuable than the standard liability, see if your homeowner's policy covers your valuables, get baggage insurance as part of your comprehensive travel-insurance package, or buy Travel Guard's "BagTrak" product. Don't buy insurance at the airport, where it's usually overpriced. Be sure to take any valuables or irreplaceable items with you in your carry-on luggage, because airline policies don't cover many valuables.

If your luggage is lost, immediately file a lost-luggage claim at the airport, detailing the contents. For most airlines, you must report delayed, damaged, or lost baggage within 4 hours of arrival. The airlines are required to deliver luggage, once found, directly to your house or destination free of charge.

6 Health & Safety

STAYING HEALTHY

GENERAL AVAILABILITY OF HEALTH CARE

In most of the Yucatán's resort destinations, health care meeting U.S. standards is now available. Mexico's major cities are also known for their excellent health care, although the facilities available may be sparser, and equipment older than what is available at home. Prescription medicine is broadly available at Mexico pharmacies; however, be aware that you may need a copy of your prescription, or need to obtain a prescription from a local doctor.

Mosquitoes and gnats are prevalent along the coast. Insect repellent *(repelente contra insectos)* is a must, and it's not always available in Mexico. Bring along a repellent that contains the active ingredient DEET. Avon's Skin So Soft also works extremely well. If you're sensitive to bites, pick up some antihistamine cream from a drugstore at home.

Most visitors won't ever see a scorpion *(alacrán)*. But if you're stung by one, go immediately to a doctor.

MORE SERIOUS DISEASES You shouldn't be overly concerned about tropical diseases if you stay on the normal tourist routes and don't eat street food. However, both dengue fever and cholera have appeared in Mexico in recent years. Talk to your doctor or to a medical specialist in tropical diseases about precautions you should take. You can also get medical bulletins from the **U.S. State Department** and the **Centers for Disease Control** (see "Visitor Information," earlier in this chapter). You can protect yourself by taking some simple precautions: Watch what you eat and drink; don't swim in stagnant water (ponds, slow-moving rivers, or wells); and avoid mosquito bites by covering up, using repellent, and sleeping under mosquito netting. The most dangerous areas seem to be on Mexico's west coast, away from the big resorts, which are relatively safe.

Contact the **International Association for Medical Assistance to Travelers (IAMAT; © 716/754-4883,** or 416/652-0137 in Canada; www.iamat.org) for tips on travel and health concerns in the countries you're visiting, and lists of local, English-speaking doctors.

EMERGENCY EVACUATION For extreme medical emergencies, a 24-hour air-ambulance service from the United States will fly people to American hospitals. **Global Lifeline (© 888/554-9729,** or 01-800/305-9400 in Mexico) is a 24-hour air ambulance. Several other companies offer air-evacuation services; for a list, refer to the U.S. State Department website, http://travel.state.gov/medical.html.

SAFETY

CRIME I have lived and traveled in Mexico for over more than a dozen years, have never had any serious trouble, and rarely feel suspicious of anyone or any situation. You will probably feel physically safer in most Mexican cities and villages than in any comparable place at home. Most crimes are robberies or motivated by jealousy. Random, violent, or serial crime is essentially unheard of in Mexico. However, it should be noted that crime, including taxi robberies, kidnappings, and highway carjackings, is on the rise. The most severe problems have been concentrated in Mexico City, but isolated incidents have also occurred in Cancún, Ixtapa, Baja, and even traditionally tranquil Puerto Escondido.

Precautions are necessary, but travelers should be realistic. Common sense is essential. You can generally trust people whom you approach for help or directions—but be wary of anyone who approaches you offering the same. The more insistent the person is, the more cautious you should be. You are much more likely to meet kind and helpful Mexicans than you are to encounter those set on thievery and deceit. Check the **U.S. State Department advisory** (http://travel.state.gov) before you travel for any notable "hot spots." For more information, see "Fast Facts: Emergencies" later in this chapter.

BRIBES & SCAMS As is the case around the world, there are the occasional bribes and scams in Mexico, targeted at people believed to be naive—such as the telltale tourist. For years Mexico was known as a place where bribes—called *mordidas* (bites)—were expected; however, the country is rapidly changing. Frequently, offering a bribe today, especially to a police officer, is considered an insult, and it can land you in deeper trouble.

Whatever you do, **avoid impoliteness;** under no circumstances should you insult a Latin American official. Extreme politeness, even in the face of adversity, rules Mexico. In Mexico, *gringos* have a reputation for being loud and demanding. By adopting the local custom of excessive courtesy, you'll have greater success in negotiations of any kind. Stand your ground, but do it politely.

Tips **Over-the-Counter Drugs in Mexico**

Mexican pharmacies sell antibiotics and other drugs that you'd need a prescription to buy in the States. Pharmacies also carry common over-the-counter cold, sinus, and allergy remedies, although not the broad selection we're accustomed to.

Tips What to Do If You Get Sick

It's called "travelers' diarrhea" or ***turista,*** the Spanish word for "tourist": persistent diarrhea, often accompanied by fever, nausea, and vomiting, that used to attack many travelers to Mexico. (Some in the United States call this "Montezuma's revenge," but you won't hear it called that in Mexico.) Widespread improvements in infrastructure, sanitation, and education have practically eliminated this ailment, especially in well-developed resort areas. Most travelers make a habit of drinking only bottled water, which helps to protect against unfamiliar bacteria. In resort areas, and generally throughout Mexico, only purified ice is used. If you do come down with this ailment, nothing beats Pepto Bismol, readily available in Mexico. Imodium is also available in Mexico, and many travelers use it for a quick fix. A good high-potency (or "therapeutic") vitamin supplement and even extra vitamin C can help; yogurt is good for healthy digestion.

Dehydration can quickly become life threatening, so the Public Health Service advises that you be especially careful to replace fluids and electrolytes (potassium, sodium, and the like) during a bout of diarrhea. Do this by drinking Pedialyte, a rehydration solution available at most Mexican pharmacies, or glasses of natural fruit juice (high in potassium) with a pinch of salt added. Or you can try a glass of boiled pure water with a quarter teaspoon of sodium bicarbonate (baking soda) added.

How to Prevent It: The U.S. Public Health Service recommends the following measures for preventing travelers' diarrhea: **Drink only purified water** (boiled water; canned or bottled carbonated beverages, beer, wine). **Choose food carefully.** In general, avoid salads (except in first-class restaurants), uncooked vegetables, and unpasteurized milk or milk products (including cheese). Choose food that is freshly cooked and still hot. In addition, something as simple as **clean hands** can go a long way toward preventing *turista.*

7 Specialized Travel Resources

FAMILY TRAVEL

Mexicans will warmly welcome and cater to your children. Many parents were reluctant to bring young children into Mexico in the past, primarily due to health concerns. I can't think of a better place to introduce children to the exciting adventure of exploring a different culture. One of the best places for children in Mexico is Cancún, with its array of theme parks and attractions. Hotels can often arrange for a babysitter. Some hotels in the moderate-to-luxury range have small playgrounds and pools for children and hire caretakers who plan special activity programs during the day. Few budget hotels offer these amenities.

Before leaving, you should check with your doctor to get advice on medications to take along. Disposable diapers cost about the same in Mexico but are of poorer quality. You can get Huggies Supreme and Pampers identical to the ones sold in the United States, but at a higher price. Many stores sell Gerber's baby foods. Dry cereals, powdered formulas, baby bottles, and purified water are all easily available in midsize and large cities or resorts.

Cribs, however, may present a problem; only the largest and most luxurious hotels provide them. However, rollaway beds to accommodate children staying in the room with parents are often available. Child seats or high chairs at restaurants are common, and most restaurants will go out of their way to accommodate your child.

You might want to consider bringing your own car seat; they are not readily available for rent in Mexico.

For more resources, see **Family Travel Forum** (www.familytravelforum.com), a comprehensive site that offers customized trip planning; and **Traveling Internationally with Your Kids** (www.travelwithyourkids.com), a comprehensive site offering sound advice for long-distance and international travel with children.

TRAVELERS WITH DISABILITIES

Mexico may seem like a giant obstacle course to travelers in wheelchairs or on crutches. At airports, you may encounter steep stairs before finding a well-hidden elevator or escalator—if one exists. Airlines will often arrange wheelchair assistance for passengers to the baggage area. Porters are generally available to help with luggage at airports and large bus stations, once you've cleared baggage claim.

Mexican airports are upgrading their services, but it is not uncommon to board from a remote position, meaning you either descend stairs to a bus that ferries you to the plane, which you board by climbing stairs, or you walk across the tarmac to your plane and ascend the stairs. Deplaning presents the same problem in reverse.

Escalators (and there aren't many) are often out of order. Stairs without handrails abound. Few restrooms are equipped for travelers with disabilities; when one is available, access to it may be through a narrow passage that won't accommodate a wheelchair or a person on crutches. Many deluxe hotels (the most expensive) now have rooms with bathrooms for people with disabilities. Those traveling on a budget should stick with one-story hotels or hotels with elevators. Even so, there will probably still be obstacles somewhere. Generally speaking, no matter where you are, someone will lend a hand, although you may have to ask for it. **Access-Able Travel Source** (✆ **303/232-2979**; www.access-able.com) offers extensive access information and advice for traveling around the world with disabilities.

SENIOR TRAVEL

Mexico is a popular country for retirees. For decades, North Americans have been living indefinitely in Mexico by returning to the border and recrossing with a new tourist permit every 6 months. Mexican immigration officials have caught on and now limit the maximum time in the country to 6 months within any year. This is to encourage even partial residents to comply with the proper documentation procedures. ***AIM,*** Apdo. Postal 31–70, 45050 Guadalajara, Jal., is a well-written, informative newsletter for prospective retirees. Subscriptions are $18 to the United States and $21 to Canada. Back issues are three for $5.

Recommended publications offering travel resources and discounts for seniors include: the quarterly magazine ***Travel 50 & Beyond*** (www.travel50andbeyond.com); ***Travel Unlimited: Uncommon Adventures for the Mature Traveler*** (Avalon); and ***101 Tips for Mature Travelers,*** available from Grand Circle Travel (✆ **800/221-2610** or 617/350-7500; www.gct.com).

GAY & LESBIAN TRAVELERS

Mexico is a conservative country, with deeply rooted Catholic religious traditions. Public displays of same-sex affection are rare and still considered shocking for men, especially outside urban or resort areas. Women in Mexico frequently walk hand in hand, but anything more would cross the boundary of acceptability. However, gay and lesbian travelers are generally treated with respect and should not experience any harassment, assuming that the appropriate regard is given to local culture and customs.

Tips Advice for Female Travelers

As a female traveling alone, I can tell you firsthand that I feel safer traveling in Mexico than in the United States. But I use the same common-sense precautions I follow traveling anywhere else in the world and am alert to what's going on around me.

Mexicans in general, and men in particular, are nosy about single travelers, especially women. Movies and television shows exported from the United States have created an image of sexually promiscuous North American women. If you're bothered by someone, don't try to be polite—just leave or head into a public place. If taxi drivers or anyone else with whom you don't want to become friendly asks about your marital status, family, and so forth, my advice is to make up a set of answers (regardless of the truth): "I'm married, I'm traveling with friends, and I have three children." Saying you are single and traveling alone may send the wrong message. Check out the award-winning website **Journeywoman** (www.journeywoman.com), a "real life" women's travel information network where you can sign up for a free e-mail newsletter and get advice on everything from etiquette and dress to safety; or the travel guide ***Safety and Security for Women Who Travel*** by Sheila Swan and Peter Laufer (Travelers' Tales, Inc.), offering common-sense tips on safe travel.

The International Gay and Lesbian Travel Association (**IGLTA; ✆ 800/448-8550** or 954/776-2626; www.iglta.org) is the trade association for the gay and lesbian travel industry, and offers an online directory of gay- and lesbian-friendly travel businesses; go to their website and click on "Members."

8 Planning Your Trip Online

The "big three" online travel agencies, **Expedia.com, Travelocity.com,** and **Orbitz.com,** sell most of the air tickets bought on the Internet. (Canadian travelers should try expedia.ca and Travelocity.ca; U.K. residents can go for expedia.co.uk and opodo.co.uk.) Each has different business deals with the airlines and may offer different fares on the same flights, so it's wise to shop around.

Expedia and Travelocity will also send you **e-mail notification** when a cheap fare becomes available to your favorite destination. Of the smaller travel agency websites, **SideStep** (www.sidestep.com) has gotten the best reviews from Frommer's authors. It's a browser add-on that purports to "search 140 sites at once," but in reality only beats competitors' fares as often as other sites do.

Also remember to check **airline websites,** especially those for low-fare carriers such as Southwest, STS, or whose fares are often misreported or simply missing from travel agency websites. Even with major airlines, you can often shave a few bucks from a fare by booking directly through the airline and avoiding a travel agency's transaction fee. But you'll get these discounts only by **booking online:** Most airlines now offer online-only fares that even their phone agents know nothing about. For the websites of airlines that fly to and from Cancún, go to "Getting There," below.

Great **last-minute deals** are available through free weekly e-mail services provided directly by the airlines. Most of these are announced on Tuesday or Wednesday and must be purchased online. Most are only valid for travel that weekend, but some (such as Southwest's) can be booked weeks or months in advance. Sign up for weekly e-mail alerts at airline websites or check mega-sites that compile comprehensive lists of last-minute specials, such as **Smarter Travel** (smartertravel.com). For last-minute trips, **site59.com** and **lastminutetravel.com** in the U.S. and **lastminute.com** in Europe often have better air-and-hotel package deals than the major-label sites. A website listing numerous bargain sites and airlines around the world is **www.itravelnet.com**.

If you're willing to give up some control over your flight details, use what is called an **"opaque" fare service** like **Priceline** (www.priceline.com; www.priceline.co.uk for Europeans) or its smaller competitor **Hotwire** (www.hotwire.com). Both offer rock-bottom prices in exchange for travel on a "mystery airline" at a mysterious time of day, often with a mysterious change of planes en route. The mystery airlines are all major, well-known carriers—and the possibility of being sent from Philadelphia to Chicago via Tampa is remote; the airlines' routing computers have gotten a lot better than they used to be. But your chances of getting a 6am or 11pm flight are pretty high. Hotwire tells you flight prices before you buy; Priceline usually has better deals than Hotwire, but you have to play their "name our price" game. If you're new at this, the helpful folks at **BiddingForTravel** (www.biddingfortravel.com) do a good job of demystifying Priceline's prices and strategies. Priceline and Hotwire are great for flights within North America and between the U.S. and

Europe. But for flights to other parts of the world, consolidators will almost always beat their fares. ***Note:*** In 2004 Priceline added non-opaque service to its roster. You now have the option to pick exact flights, times, and airlines from a list of offers—or opt to bid on opaque fares as before.

For much more about airfares and savvy air-travel tips and advice, pick up a copy of ***Frommer's Fly Safe, Fly Smart*** (Wiley Publishing, Inc.).

SURFING FOR HOTELS

Shopping online for hotels is generally done one of two ways: by booking through the hotel's own website or through an independent booking agency (or a fare-service agency like Priceline; see below). These Internet hotel agencies have multiplied in mind-boggling numbers of late, competing for the business of millions of consumers surfing for accommodations around the world. This competitiveness can be a boon to consumers who have the patience

Frommers.com: The Complete Travel Resource

For an excellent travel-planning resource, we highly recommend **Frommers.com** (www.frommers.com), voted Best Travel Site by *PC Magazine.* We're a little biased, of course, but we guarantee that you'll find the travel tips, reviews, monthly vacation giveaways, bookstore, and online-booking capabilities thoroughly indispensable. Among the special features are our popular **Destinations** section, where you'll get expert travel tips, hotel and dining recommendations, and advice on the sights to see for more than 3,500 destinations around the globe; the **Frommers.com Newsletter,** with the latest deals, travel trends, and money-saving secrets; our **Community** area featuring **Message Boards,** where Frommer's readers post queries and share advice (sometimes even our authors show up to answer questions); and our **Photo Center,** where you can post and share vacation tips. When your research is done, the **Online Reservations System** (www.frommers.com/book_a_trip) takes you to Frommer's preferred online partners for booking your vacation at affordable prices.

and time to shop and compare the online sites for good deals—but shop they must, for prices can vary considerably from site to site. And keep in mind that hotels at the top of a site's listing may be there for no other reason than that they paid money to get the placement.

Of the "big three" sites, **Expedia** offers a long list of special deals and "virtual tours" or photos of available rooms so you can see what you're paying for (a feature that helps counter the claims that the best rooms are often held back from bargain booking websites). **Travelocity** posts unvarnished customer reviews and ranks its properties according to the AAA rating system. Also reliable are **Hotels.com** and **Quikbook.com.** An excellent free program, **TravelAxe** (www.travelaxe.net), can help you search multiple hotel sites at once, even ones you may never have heard of—and conveniently lists the total price of the room, including the taxes and service charges. Another booking site, **Travelweb** (www.travelweb.com), is partly owned by the hotels it represents (including the Hilton, Hyatt, and Starwood chains) and is therefore plugged directly into the hotels' reservations systems—unlike independent online agencies, which have to fax or e-mail reservation requests to the hotel, a good portion of which get misplaced in the shuffle. More than once, travelers have arrived at the hotel, only to be told that they have no reservation. To be fair, many of the major sites are undergoing improvements in service and ease of use, and Expedia will soon be able to plug directly into the reservations systems of many hotel chains—none of which can be bad news for consumers. In the meantime, it's a good idea to **get a confirmation number** and **make a printout** of any online booking transaction.

In the opaque website category, **Priceline** and **Hotwire** are even better for hotels than for airfares; with both, you're allowed to pick the neighborhood and quality level of your hotel before offering up your money. Priceline's hotel product even covers Europe and Asia, though it's much better at getting five-star lodging for three-star prices than at finding anything at the bottom of the scale. On the downside, many hotels stick Priceline guests in their least desirable rooms. Be sure to go to the BiddingForTravel website (see above) before bidding on a hotel room on Priceline; it features a fairly up-to-date list of hotels that Priceline uses in major cities. For both Priceline and Hotwire, you pay upfront, and the fee is nonrefundable. ***Note:*** Some hotels do not provide loyalty program credits or points or other frequent-stay amenities when you book a room through opaque online services.

Tips **The Best Websites for Cancún**

- **All About Cancún. (www.cancunmx.com)** This site is a good place to start. There's a database of answers to the most commonly asked questions, called "The Online Experts," with input from lots of recent travelers to the region.
- **Cancún Convention & Visitors Bureau. (http://gocancun.com)** This official site of the Cancún Convention and Visitor's Bureau lists excellent information on events and area attractions. Its hotel guide is complete and offers online booking.
- **Cancún Online. (www.cancun.com)** This comprehensive guide has lots of information about things to do and see in Cancún, with most details provided by paying advertisers. Highlights include forums, live chat, property-swap, bulletin boards, plus information on local Internet access, news, and events. You can even reserve a golf tee time or conduct wedding planning online.
- **Cancún Travel Guide. (www.go2cancun.com)** This group specializing in online information about Mexico has put together an excellent resource for Cancún rentals, hotels, and area attractions. Note that only paying advertisers are listed, but you'll find most of the major players here.

SURFING FOR RENTAL CARS

For booking rental cars online, the best deals are usually at rental-car company websites, although all the major online travel agencies also offer rental-car reservations services. Priceline and Hotwire work well for rental cars, too; the only "mystery" is which major rental company you get, and for most travelers the difference between Hertz, Avis, and Budget is negligible.

9 Getting There

BY PLANE

The airline situation in Mexico is changing rapidly, with many new regional carriers offering scheduled service to areas previously not served. In addition to regularly scheduled service, charter service direct from U.S. cities to resorts is making Mexico more accessible.

THE MAJOR INTERNATIONAL AIRLINES The main airlines operating direct or nonstop flights from the United States to Cancún include **AeroCalifornia** (© 800/237-6225), **Aeromexico** (© 800/237-6639), **Air France** (© 800/237-2747), **America West** (© 800/235-9292; www.americawest.com), **American Airlines** (© 800/433-7300), **Continental** (© 800/231-0856), **Frontier Airlines** (© 800/432-1359; www.frontierairlines.com), **Lacsa** (© 800/225-2272), **Mexicana** (© 800/531-7921), **Northwest/KLM** (© 800/225-2525), **United** (© 800/241-6522), and **US Airways** (© 800/428-4322).

The main departure points in North America for international airlines are Atlanta, Chicago, Dallas/Fort Worth, Denver, Houston, Los Angeles, Las Vegas, Miami, New York, Orlando, Philadelphia, Phoenix, Raleigh/Durham, San Antonio, San Francisco, Seattle, Toronto, and Washington, D.C.

GETTING THROUGH THE AIRPORT

With the federalization of security, procedures at U.S. airports are more stable and consistent than ever. Generally, you'll be fine if you arrive at the airport **1 hour** before a domestic flight and **2 hours** before an international flight; if you show up late, tell an airline employee and she'll probably whisk you to the front of the line.

Bring a **current, government-issued photo ID** such as a driver's license or passport. Keep your ID at the ready to show at check-in, the security checkpoint, and sometimes even the gate. (Children under 18 do not need government-issued photo IDs for domestic flights, but they do for international flights to most countries.)

In 2003, the TSA phased out **gate check-in** at all U.S. airports. And **e-tickets** have made paper tickets nearly obsolete. Passengers with e-tickets can beat the ticket-counter lines by using airport **electronic kiosks** or even **online check-in** from their home computers. Online check-in involves logging on to your airline's website, accessing your reservation, and printing out your boarding pass—and the airline may even offer you bonus miles to do so! If you're using a kiosk at the airport, bring the credit card you used to book the ticket or your frequent-flier card. Print out your boarding pass from the kiosk and simply proceed to the security checkpoint with your pass and a photo ID. If you're checking bags or looking to snag an exit-row seat, you will be able to do so using most airline kiosks. Even the smaller airlines are employing the kiosk system, but always call your airline to make sure these alternatives are available. Note that at press time, these check-in services were not available at Mexico's airports, so plan on checking in the old-fashioned way—by standing in line. **Curbside check-in** is also a good way to avoid lines, although a few airlines still ban curbside check-in; call before you go.

Security checkpoint lines are getting shorter than they were during 2001 and 2002, but some doozies remain. If you have trouble standing for long periods of time, tell an airline employee; the airline will provide a wheelchair. Speed up security by **not wearing metal objects** such as big belt buckles. If you've got metallic body parts, a note from your doctor can prevent a long chat with the security screeners. Keep in mind that only **ticketed passengers** are allowed past security, except for folks escorting passengers with disabilities or children.

Federalization has stabilized **what you can carry on** and **what you can't.** The general rule is that sharp things are out, nail clippers are okay, and food and beverages must be passed through the X-ray machine—but that security screeners can't make you drink from your coffee cup. Bring food in your carry-on rather than checking it, as explosive-detection machines used on checked luggage have been known to mistake food (especially chocolate, for some reason) for bombs. Travelers in the U.S. are allowed one carry-on bag, plus a "personal item" such as a purse, briefcase, or laptop bag. Carry-on hoarders can stuff all sorts of things into a laptop bag; as long as it has a laptop in it, it's still considered a personal item. The Transportation Security Administration (TSA) has issued a list of restricted items; check its website (www.tsa.gov/public/index.jsp) for details.

Airport screeners may decide that your checked luggage needs to be searched by hand. You can now purchase luggage locks that allow screeners to open and re-lock a checked bag if hand-searching is

Travel in the Age of Bankruptcy

Airlines go bankrupt, so protect yourself by **buying your tickets with a credit card,** as the Fair Credit Billing Act guarantees that you can get your money back from the credit card company if a travel supplier goes under (and if you request the refund within 60 days of the bankruptcy). **Travel insurance** can also help, but make sure it covers against "carrier default" for your specific travel provider. And be aware that if a U.S. airline goes bust mid-trip, a 2001 federal law requires other carriers to take you to your destination (albeit on a space-available basis) for a fee of no more than $25, provided you rebook within 60 days of the cancellation.

necessary. Look for Travel Sentry certified locks at luggage or travel shops and Brookstone stores (you can buy them online at www.brookstone.com). These locks, approved by the TSA, can be opened by luggage inspectors with a special code or key. For more information on the locks, visit www.travelsentry.org. If you use something other than TSA-approved locks, your lock will be cut off your suitcase if a TSA agent needs to hand-search your luggage.

BY CAR

Driving is not the cheapest way to get to Mexico, but it is the best way to see the country. Even so, you may think twice about taking your own car south of the border once you've pondered the bureaucracy that affects foreign drivers here. One option is to rent a car for touring around a specific region when you arrive in Mexico. Rental cars in Mexico are now generally new, clean, and very well maintained. Discounts are often available for rentals of a week or longer. (See "Car Rentals," later in this chapter, for more details.)

After reading the section that follows, if you have any additional questions or want to confirm the current rules, call the nearest Mexican consulate or Mexican Government Tourist Office. Although travel insurance companies are generally helpful, they may not have the most accurate information available. To check on road conditions or to get help with any travel emergency while in Mexico, call ✆ **01/800/903-9200,** or 55/5250-0151 in Mexico City. English-speaking operators staff both numbers.

In addition, check with the **U.S. State Department** (see "Visitor Information," at the beginning of this chapter) for warnings about dangerous driving areas.

CAR DOCUMENTS To drive your car into Mexico, you'll need a **temporary car-importation permit,** which is granted after you provide a strictly required list of documents (see below). The permit can be obtained through Banco del Ejército *(Banjercito)* officials, who have a desk, booth, or office at the Mexican Customs *(Aduana)* building after you cross the border into Mexico. Insurance companies such as AAA and Sanborn's used to be able to issue this permit; however, they may no longer do so.

The following requirements for border crossing were accurate at press time:

- **A valid driver's license,** issued outside Mexico.
- **Current, original car registration and a copy of the original car title.** If the registration or title is in more than one name and not all the named people are traveling with you, then a

Tips Carrying Car Documents

You must carry your temporary car-importation permit, tourist permit (see the earlier section, "Entry Requirements"), and, if you purchased it, your proof of Mexican car insurance (discussed later in this chapter) in the car at all times. The temporary car-importation permit papers will be issued for 6 to 12 months; the tourist permit is usually issued for 30 days. It's a good idea to overestimate the time you'll spend in Mexico so that if something unforeseen happens and you have to (or want to) stay longer, you'll avoid the hassle of getting your papers extended. Whatever you do, don't overstay either permit. Doing so invites heavy fines or confiscation of your vehicle, which will not be returned. Remember also that 6 months does not necessarily work out to be 180 days.

notarized letter from the absent person(s) authorizing use of the vehicle for the trip is required; have it ready just in case. The car registration and your credit card must be in the same name.

- **A valid international major credit card.** With a credit card, you are required to pay only a $22.50 car-importation fee. The credit card must be in the same name as the car registration. If you do not have a major credit card (American Express, Diners Club, MasterCard, or Visa), you will have to post a bond or make a deposit equal to the value of the vehicle. Check cards are not accepted.
- **Original immigration documentation.** This will be either your tourist permit (FMT) or the original immigration booklet, FM2 or FM3, if you hold this more permanent status.
- **A signed declaration promising to return to your country of origin with the vehicle.** This form *(Carta Promesa de Retorno)* is provided by *Banjercito* officials at the border. There's no charge. The form does not stipulate that you must return through the same border entry that you came through on your way south.
- **Temporary Importation Application.** By signing this form, you state that you are only temporarily importing the car for your personal use and that you will not sell the vehicle. This is to help regulate the entry and restrict the resale of unauthorized cars and trucks. Vehicles in the U.S. are much less expensive and for years have been brought into Mexico for resale.

If you receive your documentation at the border, Mexican officials will make two copies of everything and charge you for the copies. For up-to-the-minute information, a great source is the Customs office in Nuevo Laredo (Módulo de Importación Temporal de Automóviles, Aduana Nuevo Laredo; © **52-867/712-2071**).

Important reminder: Someone else may drive the car, but the person (or a relative of the person) whose name appears on the car-importation permit must *always* be in the car at the same time. (If stopped by police, a nonregistered family member driver driving without the registered driver must be prepared to prove familial relationship to the registered driver—no joke.) Violation of this rule makes the car subject to impoundment and the driver subject to imprisonment or a fine. You can drive a car with foreign license plates only if you have an international (non-Mexican) driver's license.

MEXICAN AUTO INSURANCE Auto liability insurance is legally required in Mexico. U.S. insurance is invalid in Mexico; to be insured in Mexico, you must purchase Mexican insurance. An accident involving any party without insurance may be sent to jail and have his or her car impounded until all claims are settled. This is true even if you just drive across the border to spend the day. U.S. companies that broker Mexican insurance are commonly found at the border crossing, and several quote daily rates.

You can also buy car insurance through **Sanborn's Mexico Insurance,** P.O. Box 52840, 2009 S. 10th, McAllen, TX 78505-2840 (© **800/222-0158** or 956/686-3601; fax 956/686-0732; www.sanbornsinsurance.com). The company has offices at all U.S. border crossings. Its policies cost the same as the competition's, but you get legal coverage (attorney and bail bonds, if needed) and a detailed mile-by-mile guide for your proposed route. Most of the Sanborn's border offices are open from Monday to Friday, and a few are staffed on Saturday and Sunday. The American Automobile Association (AAA) also sells insurance. Another good source is www.mexico-car-insurance.com.

RETURNING TO THE UNITED STATES WITH YOUR CAR You must return the car papers that you obtained when you entered Mexico when you cross back with your car, or at some point within 180 days. (You can cross as many times as you want within the 180 days.) If the documents aren't returned, heavy fines are imposed ($250 for each 15 days late), and your car may be impounded and confiscated or you may be jailed if you return to Mexico. You can return the car documents only to a *Banjercito* official on duty at the

Mexican Customs *(Aduana)* building before you cross back into the United States. Some border cities have *Banjercito* officials on duty 24 hours a day, but others do not; some also do not have Sunday hours. On the U.S. side, Customs agents may or may not inspect your car from stem to stern.

BY SHIP

Numerous cruise lines serve the Mexican Caribbean. Trips might cruise from Miami to the Caribbean (which often includes stops in Cancún, Playa del Carmen, and Cozumel). Several cruise-tour specialists arrange substantial discounts on unsold cabins if you're willing to take off at the last minute. One such company is **The Cruise Line,** 150 NW 168th St., North Miami Beach, FL 33169 (✆ **800/777-0707** or 305/521-2200).

BY BUS

Greyhound-Trailways (or its affiliates) offers service from around the United States to the Mexican border, where passengers disembark, cross the border, and buy a ticket for travel into the interior of Mexico. At many border crossings there are scheduled buses from the U.S. bus station to the Mexican bus station.

10 Packages for the Independent Traveler

Before you start your search for the lowest airfare, you may want to consider booking your flight as part of a travel package. Package tours are not the same thing as escorted tours. Package tours are simply a way to buy the airfare, accommodations, and other elements of your trip (such as car rentals, airport transfers, and sometimes even activities) at the same time and often at discounted prices—kind of like one-stop shopping.

For popular destinations such as Cancún and the Yucatán's other beach resorts, they're often the smart way to go, because they can save you a ton of money. In many cases, a package that includes airfare, hotel, and transportation to and from the airport will cost you less than the hotel alone if you booked it yourself. That's because tour operators buy packages in bulk and resell them to the public.

You can buy a package at any time of the year, but the best deals usually coincide with high season—from mid-December to April—when demand is at its peak, and companies are more confident about filling planes. You might think that package rates would be better during low season, when room rates and airfares plunge. But the key is air access, which is much easier during the winter. Packages vary widely, with some companies offering a better class of hotels than others. Some offer the same hotels for lower prices. Some offer flights on scheduled airlines, while others book charters. In some packages, your choices of accommodations and travel days may be limited.

You are often required to make a large payment up front. On the plus side, packages can save you money, offering group prices but allowing for independent travel. Some even let you to add on a few guided excursions or escorted day trips (also at prices lower than if you booked them yourself) without booking an entirely escorted tour.

Tips Before You Book a Package

- **Read the fine print.** Make sure you know *exactly* what's included in the price you're being quoted—and what's not. Ask whether airport departure fees and taxes, for example, are included in the total cost.
- **Don't compare Mayas and Aztecs.** When you're looking over different packagers, compare the deals that they're offering on similar properties. Most packagers offer bigger savings on some hotels than on others.
- **Know what you're getting yourself into—and if you can get yourself out of it.** Before you commit to a package, make sure you know how much flexibility you have.
- **Check with the Better Business Bureau** in the city where the company is based, or go online at www.bbb.org if you're unsure about the pedigree of a smaller packager. If a packager won't tell you where they're based, don't fly with them.
- **Ask about the accommodations choices** and prices for each. Then look up the hotels' reviews in a Frommer's guide and check their rates online for your specific dates of travel.
- **Find out what type of room you're getting.** If you need a certain type of room, ask for it; don't take whatever is thrown your way. Request a nonsmoking room, a quiet room, a room with a view, or whatever you fancy.
- **Use your best judgment.** Stay away from fly-by-nights and shady packagers. Go with a reputable firm with a proven track record. This is where your travel agent can come in handy.

RECOMMENDED PACKAGERS

In addition to the companies below, several big **online travel agencies**—Expedia, Travelocity, Orbitz, Site59, and Lastminute.com—also do a brisk business in packages. The biggest **hotel chains and resorts** also sell packages. To take advantage of these offers, contact your travel agent or call the hotels directly.

Travel packages are also listed in the travel section of your local Sunday newspaper. Or check ads in the national travel magazines such as *Arthur Frommer's Budget Travel Magazine, Travel & Leisure, National Geographic Traveler,* and *Condé Nast Traveler.*

- **Mexico Travel Net** (© **800/511-4848;** www.mexicotravelnet.com) specializes in vacation packages to Mexican beach resorts and offers last-minute specials.
- **Vacation Hot Line** (© **800/325-2485;** www.vacationhotline.net) sells packages from the popular Apple and Funjet vacation wholesalers, as well as last-minute air-only or package bargains. Once you find your deal, you'll need to call to make booking arrangements.
- **Aeromexico Vacations** (© **800/245-8585;** www.aeromexico.com) offers year-round packages to almost every destination it serves, including Acapulco, Cancún, Cozumel, Ixtapa/Zihuatanejo, Los Cabos, and Puerto Vallarta. Aeromexico has a large (more than 100) selection of resorts in these destinations and more, in a variety of price ranges. The best deals are from Houston, Dallas, San Diego, Los Angeles, Miami, and New York, in that order.
- **Alaska Airlines Vacations** (© **800/468-2248;** www.alaskaair.com) sells packages to Ixtapa/Zihuatanejo, Los Cabos, Manzanillo/Costa Alegre, Mazatlán, and Puerto Vallarta. Alaska flies direct from Los Angeles, San Diego, San Jose, San Francisco, Seattle, Vancouver, Anchorage, and Fairbanks. The website offers unpublished discounts that are not available through the phone operators.
- **American Airlines Vacations** (© **800/321-2121;** www.aavacations.com) has year-round deals to Acapulco, Cancún, the Riviera Maya, Guadalajara, Los Cabos, Mexico City, and Puerto Vallarta. You don't have to fly with American if you can get a better deal on another airline; land-only packages include hotel, hotel tax, and airport transfers. American's hubs to Mexico are Dallas/Fort Worth, Chicago, and Miami. The website

offers unpublished discounts that are not available through the operators.

- **America West Vacations** (✆ **800/356-6611;** www.americawestvacations.com) has deals to Acapulco, Guadalajara, Ixtapa, Mazatlán, Manzanillo, Mexico City, Los Cabos, and Puerto Vallarta, mostly from its Phoenix gateway. Many packages to Los Cabos include car rentals. The website offers discounted featured specials that are not available through the operators. You can also book hotels without air by calling the toll-free number.
- **Apple Vacations** (✆ **800/365-2775;** www.applevacations.com) offers inclusive packages to all the beach resorts, and has the largest choice of hotels in Acapulco, Cancún, Cozumel, Huatulco, Ixtapa, Loreto, Los Cabos, Manzanillo, Mazatlán, Puerto Vallarta, and the Riviera Maya. Scheduled carriers for the air portion include American, United, Mexicana, Delta, US Airways, Reno Air, Alaska Airlines, Aero California, and Aeromexico. Apple perks include baggage handling and the services of a company representative at major hotels.
- **Classic Custom Vacations** (✆ **800/635-1333;** www.classiccustomvacations.com) specializes in package vacations to Mexico's finest luxury resorts. It combines discounted first-class and economy airfare on American, Continental, Mexicana, Alaska, America West, and Delta with stays at the most exclusive hotels in Cancún, the Riviera Maya, Mérida, Oaxaca, Guadalajara, Mexico City, Puerto Vallarta, Mazatlán, Costa Alegre, Manzanillo, Ixtapa/Zihuatanejo, Acapulco, Huatulco, and Los Cabos. In many cases, packages also include meals, airport transfers, and upgrades. The prices are not for bargain hunters but for those who seek luxury, nicely packaged.
- **Continental Vacations** (✆ **800/301-3800;** www.covacations.com) has year-round packages to Cancún, Cozumel, Puerto Vallarta, Cabo San Lucas, Acapulco, Ixtapa, Mazatlán, Mexico City, and Guadalajara. The best deals are from Houston; Newark, N.J.; and Cleveland. You must fly Continental. The Internet deals offer savings not available elsewhere.
- **Delta Vacations** (✆ **800/221-6666;** www.deltavacations.com) has year-round packages to Acapulco, Los Cabos, Cozumel, and Cancún. Atlanta is the hub, so expect the best prices from there.
- **Funjet Vacations** (book through any travel agent; www.funjet.com for general information) is one of the largest vacation

packagers in the United States. Funjet has packages to Acapulco, Cancún, Cozumel, the Riviera Maya, Huatulco, Los Cabos, Mazatlán, Ixtapa, and Puerto Vallarta. You can choose a charter or fly on American, Continental, Delta, Aeromexico, US Airways, Alaska Air, or United.

- **GOGO Worldwide Vacations** (✆ **888/636-3942;** www.gogowwv.com) has trips to all the major beach destinations, including Acapulco, Cancún, Mazatlán, Puerto Vallarta, and Los Cabos. It offers several exclusive deals from higher-end hotels. Book through any travel agent.
- **Mexicana Vacations,** or MexSeaSun Vacations (✆ **800/531-9321;** www.mexicana.com) offers getaways to all the resorts. Mexicana operates daily direct flights from Los Angeles to Los Cabos, Mazatlán, Cancún, Puerto Vallarta, Manzanillo, and Ixtapa/Zihuatanejo.
- **Online Vacation Mall** (✆ **800/839-9851;** www.onlinevacationmall.com) allows you to search for and book packages offered by a number of tour operators and airlines to Acapulco, Cancún, Cozumel, Guaymas, Huatulco, Ixtapa/Zihuatanejo, La Paz, Los Cabos, Puerto Vallarta, the Riviera Maya, Mazatlán, and Mexico City.
- **Pleasant Mexico Holidays** (✆ **800/448-3333;** www.pleasantholidays.com) is one of the largest vacation packagers in the United States, with hotels in Acapulco, Cancún, Cozumel, Ixtapa/Zihuatanejo, Los Cabos, Mazatlán, and Puerto Vallarta.

REGIONAL PACKAGERS

From the East Coast: Liberty Travel (✆ **888/271-1584;** www.libertytravel.com), one of the biggest packagers in the Northeast, often runs a full-page ad in the Sunday papers, with frequent Mexico specials. You won't get much in the way of service, but you will get a good deal.

From the West: Suntrips (✆ **800/SUNTRIPS,** or 800/786-8747 for departures within 14 days; www.suntrips.com) is one of the largest West Coast packagers for Mexico, with departures from San Francisco and Denver; regular charters to Cancún, Cozumel, Los Cabos and Puerto Vallarta; and a large selection of hotels.

From the Southwest: Town and Country (book through travel agents) packages regular deals to Los Cabos, Mazatlán, Puerto Vallarta, Ixtapa, Manzanillo, Cancún, Cozumel, and Acapulco with America West from the airline's Phoenix and Las Vegas gateways.

Finds Out-of-the-Ordinary Places to Stay

Mexico lends itself beautifully to the concept of small, private hotels in idyllic settings. They vary in style from grandiose estate to palm-thatched bungalow. **Mexico Boutique Hotels** (www.mexicoboutiquehotels.com) specializes in smaller places to stay with a high level of personal attention and service. Most options have less than 50 rooms, and the accommodations consist of entire villas, *casitas,* bungalows, or a combination. The Yucatán is especially noted for the luxury haciendas throughout the peninsula.

11 The Active Traveler

Mexico has numerous **golf** courses, especially in the resort areas; Cancún's offerings are excellent. Visitors can enjoy **tennis, waterskiing, surfing, bicycling,** and **horseback riding. Scuba diving** is excellent off the Yucatán's Caribbean coast.

Unfortunately, most of Mexico's **national parks** and **nature reserves** are understaffed or unstaffed.

OUTDOORS ORGANIZATIONS & TOUR OPERATORS

AMTAVE, or Asociación Mexicana de Turismo de Aventura y Ecoturismo, A.C. (✆ **800/509-7678;** www.amtave.org), is an association of eco- and adventure tour operators. It publishes an annual catalog of participating firms, and all its offerings must meet criteria for security, quality, and guide training, as well as for sustainability of natural and cultural environments.

The Archaeological Conservancy, 5301 Central Ave. NE, Suite 402, Albuquerque, NM 87108 (✆ **505/266-1540;** www.americanarchaeology.com/tour.html), presents one trip to Mexico per year led by an expert, usually an archaeologist. The trips change from year to year and space is limited; make reservations early.

Mexico Travel Link Ltd., 300–3665 Kingsway, Vancouver, BC V5R 5W2 Canada (✆ **604/454-9044;** fax 604/454-9088; www.mexicotravel.net), offers cultural, sports, and adventure tours to the Maya Route and other destinations.

Trek America, P.O. Box 189, Rockaway, NJ 07866 (✆ **800/221-0596** or 973/983-1144; fax 973/983-8551; www.trekamerica.com), organizes lengthy, active trips that combine trekking, hiking, van transportation, and camping in the Yucatán, Chiapas, Oaxaca, Copper Canyon, and Mexico's Pacific coast.

12 Getting Around

An important note: If your travel schedule depends on an important connection—say, a plane trip between points, or a ferry or bus connection—use the telephone numbers in this book or other information resources mentioned here to find out if the connection you are depending on is still available. Although we've done our best to provide accurate information, transportation schedules can and do change.

BY PLANE

To fly from point to point within Mexico, you'll rely on Mexican airlines. Mexico has two privately owned large national carriers: **Mexicana** (✆ **800/366-5400,** toll-free inside Mexico), and **Aeromexico** (✆ **800/021-4000,** toll-free inside Mexico), in addition to several up-and-coming regional carriers. Mexicana and Aeromexico both offer extensive connections to the United States as well as within Mexico.

Several of the regional carriers are operated by or can be booked through Mexicana or Aeromexico. Regional carriers are **AeroCaribe** (see Mexicana), **Aerolitoral** (see Aeromexico), and **Aero Mar** (see Mexicana). The regional carriers are expensive, but they go to difficult-to-reach places. In each appropriate section of this book, we've mentioned regional carriers with all pertinent telephone numbers.

Because major airlines can book some regional carriers, read your ticket carefully to see if your connecting flight is on one of these smaller carriers—they may leave from a different airport or check in at a different counter.

AIRPORT TAXES Mexico charges an airport tax on all departures. Passengers leaving the country on an international departure pay $18, in dollars or the peso equivalent. It has become a common practice to include this departure tax in your ticket price, but double-check to make sure so you're not caught by surprise at the airport upon leaving. Taxes on each domestic departure that you make within Mexico are around $13, unless you're on a connecting flight and have already paid at the start of the flight, in which case you shouldn't be charged again.

Mexico also charges an additional $18 "tourism tax," the proceeds of which go into a tourism promotional fund. Your ticket price may not include it, so be sure to have enough money to pay it at the airport upon departure.

RECONFIRMING FLIGHTS Although Mexican airlines say it's not necessary to reconfirm a flight, it's still a good practice. To avoid getting bumped on popular, possibly overbooked flights, check in for international flights the required hour and a half before travel.

BY CAR

Most Mexican roads are not up to U.S. standards of smoothness, hardness, width of curve, grade of hill, or safety marking, with the exception of the roads in and around Cancún. Driving at night is dangerous—the roads are rarely lit; trucks, carts, pedestrians, and bicycles usually have no lights; and you can hit potholes, animals, rocks, dead ends, or bridges out with no warning.

The spirited style of Mexican driving sometimes requires super vision and reflexes. Be prepared for new customs, as when a truck driver flips on his left turn signal when there's not a crossroad for miles. He's probably telling you the road's clear ahead for you to pass—after all, he's in a better position to see than you are. Another custom that's very important to respect is **how to make a left turn.** Never turn left by stopping in the middle of a highway with your left signal on. Instead, pull off the highway onto the right shoulder, wait for traffic to clear, and then proceed across the road.

GASOLINE There's one government-owned brand of gas and one gasoline station name throughout the country—**Pemex (Petroleras Mexicanas).** There are two types of gas in Mexico: *magna,* an 87-octane unleaded gas, and premium 93 octane. In Mexico, fuel and oil are sold by the liter, which is slightly more than a quart (40 liters equals about 10½ gal.). Many franchise Pemex stations have bathroom facilities and convenience stores—a great improvement over the old ones.

Important note: No credit cards are accepted for gas purchases.

TOLL ROADS Mexico charges some of the highest tolls in the world for its network of new toll roads; as a result, they are rarely used. Generally speaking, using the toll roads will cut travel time between destinations. Older toll-free roads are generally in good condition, but travel times are generally longer because the roads tend to be mountainous and clotted with slow-moving trucks.

BREAKDOWNS If your car breaks down on the road, help might already be on the way. Radio-equipped green repair trucks operated by uniformed English-speaking officers patrol the major highways during daylight hours to aid motorists in trouble. These

"Green Angels" will perform minor repairs and adjustments for free, but you pay for parts and materials.

Your best guide to repair shops is the Yellow Pages. For specific makes and shops that repair cars, look under "Automóviles y Camiones: Talleres de Reparación y Servicio"; auto-parts stores are listed under "Refacciones y Accesorios para Automóviles." To find a mechanic on the road, look for a sign that says TALLER MECANICO.

Flat tires are repaired at places called "vulcanizadora" or "llantera"; it is common to find such places open 24 hours a day on the most traveled highways. Even if the place looks empty, chances are good that you will find someone who can help you fix a flat.

MINOR ACCIDENTS When possible, many Mexicans drive away from minor accidents or try to make an immediate settlement, to avoid involving the police. If the police arrive while the involved persons are still at the scene, everyone may be locked in jail until blame is assessed. In any case, you have to settle up immediately, which may take days of red tape. Foreigners who don't speak fluent Spanish are at a distinct disadvantage when trying to explain their side of the event. Three steps may help the foreigner who doesn't want to do as the Mexicans do: If you were in your own car, notify your Mexican insurance company, whose job it is to intervene on your behalf. If you were in a rental car, notify the rental company immediately and ask how to contact the nearest adjuster. (You did buy insurance with the rental, right?) Finally, if all else fails, ask to contact the nearest Green Angel, who may be able to explain to officials that you are covered by insurance. See also "Mexican Auto Insurance" in "Getting There," earlier in this chapter.

CAR RENTALS You'll get the best price if you reserve a car at least a week in advance in the United States. U.S. car-rental firms include **Advantage** (✆ 800/777-5500 in the U.S. and Canada), **Avis** (✆ 800/331-1212 in the U.S., or 800/TRY-AVIS in Canada), **Budget** (✆ 800/527-0700 in the U.S. and Canada), **Hertz** (✆ 800/654-3131 in the U.S. and Canada), **National** (✆ 800/CAR-RENT in the U.S. and Canada), and **Thrifty** (✆ 800/367-2277 in the U.S. and Canada; www.thrifty.com), which often offers discounts for rentals in Mexico. For European travelers, **Kemwel Holiday Auto** (✆ 800/678-0678) and **Auto Europe** (✆ 800/223-5555) can arrange Mexican rentals, sometimes through other agencies. These and some local firms have offices in Mexico City and most other large Mexican cities. You'll find rental desks at airports, all major hotels, and many travel agencies.

Cars are easy to rent if you have a major credit card, are 25 or over, and have a valid driver's license and passport with you. Without a credit card, you must leave a cash deposit, usually a big one. One-way rentals are usually simple to arrange but more costly.

Car-rental costs are high in Mexico because cars are more expensive. The condition of rental cars has improved greatly over the years, however, and clean, comfortable, new cars are the norm. At press time, the basic cost of a 1-day rental of a Volkswagen Beetle with unlimited mileage (but before 17% tax and $15 daily insurance) was $44 in Cancún and $27 in Mérida. Renting by the week gives you a lower daily rate. Avis was offering a basic 7-day weekly rate for a VW Beetle (before tax or insurance) of $220 in Cancún and $160 in Mérida. Prices may be considerably higher if you rent around a major holiday.

Car-rental companies usually write up a credit card charge in U.S. dollars.

Deductibles Be careful—these vary greatly in Mexico; some are as high as $2,500, which comes out of your pocket immediately in case of car damage. Hertz's deductible is $1,000 on a VW Beetle; Avis's is $500 for the same car.

Insurance Insurance is offered in two parts: **Collision and damage** insurance covers your car and others if the accident is your fault, and **personal accident** insurance covers you and anyone in your car. Read the fine print on the back of your rental agreement, and note that insurance may be invalid if you have an accident while driving on an unpaved road.

Damage Always inspect your car carefully and note every damaged or missing item, no matter how minute, on your rental agreement, or you may be charged for it.

BY TAXI

Most airports and bus stations have *colectivos* (minibuses or minivans) or fixed-rate taxis to town or the hotel zone. The *colectivo* is always the least expensive way to go. Buy a special *colectivo* ticket from a booth that's usually located near the exit door of the main airport concourse.

Taxis are the preferred way to get around in almost all the resort areas of Mexico. Short trips within towns are generally charged by preset zones and are quite reasonable compared with U.S. rates. For longer trips or excursions to nearby cities, taxis can generally be hired for around $10 to $15 per hour, or for a negotiated daily rate.

Tips Spanish for Bus Travelers

Little English is spoken at bus stations, so come prepared with your destination written down. Then double-check the departure signs.

Even drops to different destinations—say, between Cancún and Playa del Carmen—can be arranged. A negotiated one-way price is usually much less than the cost of a rental car for a day, and service is much faster than traveling by bus. For anyone who is uncomfortable driving in Mexico, this is a convenient, comfortable alternative. A bonus is that you have a Spanish-speaking person with you in case you run into any car or road trouble. Many taxi drivers speak at least some English. Your hotel can assist you with the arrangements.

BY BUS

Bus service in the Yucatán is beginning to catch up to the high standard common elsewhere in Mexico. Buses are frequent and readily accessible and can get you to almost anywhere you want to go. They're often the only way to get from large cities to other nearby cities and small villages. Don't hesitate to ask questions if you're confused about anything.

Dozens of Mexican companies operate large, air-conditioned, Greyhound-type buses between most cities. Travel class is generally labeled second *(segunda),* first *(primera),* and deluxe *(ejecutiva),* which goes by a variety of names. The deluxe buses often have fewer seats than regular buses, show videos en route, are air-conditioned, and have few stops; some offer complimentary refreshments. Many run express from origin to final destination. These are well worth the few dollars more that you'll pay. In rural areas, buses are often of the school-bus variety, with lots of local color.

Whenever possible, it's best to buy your reserved-seat ticket, often using a computerized system, a day in advance on many long-distance routes—and especially before holidays. Schedules are fairly dependable, so be at the terminal on time for departure. Current information may be obtained from local bus stations. See the appendix for a list of helpful bus terms in Spanish.

FAST FACTS: Mexico

Abbreviations Dept. (apartments); Apdo. (post office box); Av. (*Avenida;* avenue); *c/* (*calle;* street); Calz. (*Calzada;* boulevard). "C" on faucets stands for *caliente* (hot), and "F" stands for *fría* (cold). PB *(planta baja)* means ground floor, and most buildings count the next floor up as the first floor (1).

Business Hours In general, businesses in larger cities are open between 9am and 7pm; in smaller towns, many close between 2 and 4pm. Most close on Sunday. In resort areas, it is common to find more stores open on Sundays, as well as extended business hours for shops, often until 8 or even 10pm. Bank hours are Monday to Friday from 9 or 9:30am to anywhere between 3 and 7pm. Increasingly, banks open on Saturday for at least a half-day.

Cameras & Film Film costs about the same as in the United States. Tourists who want to use a video camera or still camera at any archaeological site in Mexico and at many museums operated by the **Instituto de Antropología e Historia (INAH)** must pay $4 per video camera or still camera in their possession at each site or museum visited. Such fees are noted in the listings for specific sites and museums. Also, use of a tripod at any archaeological site in Mexico requires a permit from INAH. It's courteous to ask permission before photographing anyone, and it is never considered polite to take photos inside a church in Mexico.

Customs See "Entry Requirements & Customs," earlier in this chapter.

Doctors & Dentists Every embassy and consulate is prepared to recommend local doctors and dentists with good training and modern equipment; some of the doctors and dentists even speak English. See the list of embassies and consulates under "Embassies & Consulates," below. Hotels with a large foreign clientele are often prepared to recommend English-speaking doctors. Almost all first-class hotels in Mexico have a doctor on call.

Drug Laws To be blunt, don't use or possess illegal drugs in Mexico. Mexican officials have no tolerance for drug users, and jail is their solution, with very little hope of getting out until the sentence (usually a long one) is completed or heavy fines or bribes are paid. Remember, in Mexico the legal system assumes that you are guilty until proven innocent. (***Important note:*** It isn't uncommon to be befriended by a fellow user, only to be turned in by that "friend," who has collected a bounty.) Bring prescription drugs in their original containers. If possible, pack a copy of the original prescription with the generic name of the drug.

U.S. Customs officials are also on the lookout for diet drugs sold in Mexico but illegal in the U.S., possession of which could also land you in a U.S. jail. If you buy antibiotics over the counter (which you can do in Mexico) and still have some left, you probably won't be hassled by U.S. Customs.

Drugstores See "Pharmacies," below.

Electricity The electrical system in Mexico is 110 volts AC (60 cycles), as in the United States and Canada. However, in reality it may cycle more slowly and overheat your appliances. To compensate, select a medium or low speed for hair dryers. Many older hotels still have electrical outlets for flat two-prong plugs; you'll need an adapter for any modern electrical apparatus that has an enlarged end on one prong or that has three prongs. Many first-class and deluxe hotels have the three-holed outlets (*trifásicos* in Spanish). Those that don't may have loan adapters, but to be sure, it's always better to carry your own.

Embassies & Consulates They provide valuable lists of doctors and lawyers, as well as regulations concerning marriages in Mexico. Contrary to popular belief, your embassy cannot get you out of a Mexican jail, provide postal or banking services, or fly you home when you run out of money.

The Embassy of the **United States** in Mexico City is at Paseo de la Reforma 305, next to the Hotel María Isabel Sheraton at the corner of Río Danubio (✆ **555/080-2000,** or 555/511-9980); hours are Monday through Friday from 8:30am to 5:30pm. Visit www.usembassy-mexico.gov for addresses of the U.S. consulates inside Mexico. There are U.S. Consulates General at López Mateos 924-N, Ciudad Juárez (✆ **656/611-3000**); Progreso 175, Guadalajara (✆ **333/268-2100**); Av. Constitución 411 Pte., Monterrey (✆ **818/345-2120**); and Tapachula 96, Tijuana (✆ **664/622-7400**). In addition, there are consular agencies in Acapulco (✆ **744/469-0556**); Cabo San Lucas (✆ **624/143-3566**); Cancún (✆ **998/883-0272**); Cozumel

(© **987/872-4574**); Hermosillo (© **662/217-2375**); Ixtapa/Zihuatanejo (© **755/553-2100**); Matamoros (© **868/812-4402**); Mazatlán (© **669/916-5889**); Mérida (© **999/925-5011**); Nogales (© **631/313-4820**); Nuevo Laredo (© **867/714-0512**); Oaxaca (© **951/514-3054**); Puerto Vallarta (© **322/222-0069**); San Luis Potosí (© **444/811-7802**); and San Miguel de Allende (© **415/152-2357**).

The Embassy of **Australia** in Mexico City is at Rubén Darío 55, Col. Polanco (© **55/1101-2200;** fax 55/1101-2201). It's open Monday through Friday from 9am to 1pm.

The Embassy of **Canada** in Mexico City is at Schiller 529, Col. Polanco (© **555/724-7900**); it's open Monday through Friday from 9am to 1pm. At other times, the name of a duty officer is posted on the door. Visit **www.dfait-maeci.gc.ca** for addresses of consular agencies in Mexico. There are Canadian consulates in Acapulco (© **744/484-1305**), Cancún (© **998/883-3360**), Guadalajara (© **333/615-6215**), Mazatlán (© **669/913-7320**), Monterrey (© **818/344-2753**), Oaxaca (© **951/513-3777**), Puerto Vallarta (© **322/293-0098**), San José del Cabo (© **624/142-4333**), and Tijuana (© **664/684-0461**).

The Embassy of **New Zealand** in Mexico City is at José Luis Lagrange 103, 10th floor, Col. Los Morales Polanco (© **555/283-9460;** kiwimexico@compuserve.com.mx). It's open Monday through Friday from 8am to 3pm.

The Embassy of the **United Kingdom** in Mexico City is at Río Lerma 71, Col. Cuauhtémoc (© **555/242-8500;** www.embajadabritanica.com.mx). It's open Monday through Friday from 8:30am to 3:30pm.

The Embassy of **Ireland** in Mexico City is at Cerrada Blvd. Avila Camacho 76, 3rd floor, Col. Lomas de Chapultepec (© **555/520-5803**). It's open Monday through Friday from 9am to 5pm.

The **South African** Embassy in Mexico City is at Andres Bello 10, 9th floor, Col. Polanco (© **555/282-9260**). It's open Monday through Friday from 8am to 3:30pm.

Emergencies In case of emergency, dial 065 from any phone. The 24-hour **Tourist Help Line** in Mexico City is © **800/903-9200** or 555/250-0151. The operators don't always speak English, but they are always willing to help. The tourist legal assistance office (Procuraduría del Turista) in Mexico City (© **555/625-8153** or 555/625-8154) always has an English speaker available. Though the phones are frequently busy, they operate 24 hours.

Internet Access In large cities and resort areas, a growing number of five-star hotels offer business centers with Internet access. You'll also find cybercafes in destinations that are popular with expats and business travelers. It is very common now to find an Internet outpost even in the most remote areas. Note that many ISPs will automatically cut off your Internet connection after a specified period of time (say, 10 min.) because telephone lines are at a premium.

Legal Aid **International Legal Defense Counsel,** 111 S. 15th St., 24th Floor, Packard Building, Philadelphia, PA 19102 (✆ **215/977-9982**), is a law firm specializing in the legal difficulties of Americans abroad. See also "Embassies & Consulates" and "Emergencies," above.

Liquor Laws The legal drinking age in Mexico is 18; however, asking for ID or denying purchase is extremely rare. Grocery stores sell everything from beer and wine to national and imported liquors. You can buy liquor 24 hours a day; but during major elections dry laws often apply for as long as 72 hours in advance of the election—and those laws apply to foreign tourists as well as local residents. Mexico does not have any "open container" laws regarding transporting liquor in cars, but authorities are beginning to target drunk drivers more aggressively. It's a good idea to drive defensively.

It is not legal to drink in the street; however, many tourists do so. Use your judgment—if you are getting too drunk, you shouldn't drink in the street because you are more likely to get stopped by the police. As is the custom in Mexico, it is not so much what you do, but it is how you do it.

Lost & Stolen Property To replace a **lost passport,** contact your embassy or nearest consular agent (see "Embassies & Consulates," above). You must establish a record of your citizenship and also fill out a form requesting another **Mexican Tourist Permit** (FMT) if it, too, was lost. Without the FMT, you can't leave the country, and without an affidavit affirming your passport request and citizenship, you may have problems at Customs when you get home. It's important to clear everything up *before* trying to leave. Mexican Customs, however, may accept the police report of the loss of the tourist permit and allow you to leave.

If you lose your **wallet** anywhere outside of Mexico City, before panicking, retrace your steps—you'll be surprised at how honest people are, and you'll likely find someone trying to find you to return your wallet.

If your wallet is stolen, the police probably won't be able to recover it. Be sure to notify all of your credit card companies right away, and file a report at the nearest police precinct. Your credit card company or insurer may require a police report number or record of the loss. Most credit card companies have an emergency toll-free number to call if your card is lost or stolen; these numbers are not toll-free within Mexico (see "Telephone & Fax," below, for instructions on calling U.S. toll-free numbers). The company may be able to wire you a cash advance off your credit card immediately, and, in many places, can deliver an emergency credit card in a day or two. Visa's U.S. emergency number is ✆ **800/847-2911** or 410/581-9994. American Express cardholders and traveler's check holders should call ✆ **800/221-7282.** MasterCard holders should call ✆ **800/307-7309** or 636/722-7111. For other credit cards, call the toll-free number directory at ✆ **800/555-1212.**

If you need emergency cash over the weekend when all banks and American Express offices are closed, you can have money wired to you via **Western Union** (✆ **800/325-6000;** www.westernunion.com).

Identity theft and fraud are potential complications of losing your wallet, especially if you've lost your driver's license along with your cash and credit cards. Notify the major credit-reporting bureaus immediately; placing a fraud alert on your records may protect you against liability for criminal activity. The three major U.S. credit-reporting agencies are **Equifax** (✆ **800/766-0008;** www.equifax.com), **Experian** (✆ **888/397-3742;** www.experian.com), and **TransUnion** (✆ **800/680-7289;** www.transunion.com). Finally, if you've lost all forms of photo ID call your airline and explain the situation; they might allow you to board the plane if you have a copy of your passport or birth certificate and a copy of the police report you've filed.

Mail Postage for a postcard or letter is 1 peso; it may arrive anywhere from 1 to 6 weeks later. A registered letter costs $1.90. Sending a package can be quite expensive—the Mexican postal service charges $8 per kilo (2.20 lb.) and unreliable; it takes 2 to 6 weeks, if it arrives at all. The recommended way to send a package or important mail is through FedEx, DHL, UPS, or any other reputable international mail service.

Newspapers & Magazines There currently is no national English-language newspaper. Newspaper kiosks in larger Mexican cities carry a selection of English-language magazines.

Pharmacies *Farmacias* will sell you just about anything you want, with or without a prescription. Most pharmacies are open Monday to Saturday from 8am to 8pm. The major resort areas generally have one or two 24-hour pharmacies. Pharmacies take turns staying open during off-hours, so if you are in a smaller town and need to buy medicine after normal hours, ask for the *farmacia de turno.*

Police Outside Mexico City, especially in tourist areas such as Cancún, most police officers are very protective of international visitors.

Smoking Smoking is permitted and generally accepted in most public places, including restaurants, bars, and hotel lobbies. Nonsmoking areas and hotel rooms for nonsmokers are becoming more common in higher-end establishments, but they tend to be the exception rather than the rule.

Taxes There's a 15% IVA (value-added) tax on goods and services in most of Mexico, and it's supposed to be included in the posted price. This tax is 10% in Cancún and Cozumel. Mexico imposes an exit tax of around $18 on every foreigner leaving the country; the price of airline tickets usually includes this tax.

Telephone & Fax Mexico's telephone system is slowly but surely catching up with modern times. All telephone numbers have 10 digits. Every city and town that has telephone access has a two-digit (Mexico City, Monterrey, and Guadalajara) or three-digit (everywhere else) area code. In Mexico City, Monterrey, and Guadalajara, local numbers have eight digits; elsewhere, local numbers have seven digits. To place a local call, you do not need to dial the area code. Many fax numbers are also regular telephone numbers; ask whoever answers for the fax tone *("me da tono de fax, por favor").* Cellular phones are very popular for small businesses in resort areas and smaller communities. To call a cellular number inside the same area code, dial 044 and then the number. To dial the cellular phone from anywhere else in Mexico, first dial 01, and then the three-digit area code and the seven-digit number. To dial it from the U.S., dial 011-52, plus the three-digit area code and the seven-digit number.

The **country code** for Mexico is **52.**

To call Mexico: If you're calling Mexico from the United States:

1. Dial the international access code: 011.
2. Dial the country code: 52.
3. Dial the two- or three-digit area code, then the eight- or seven-digit number. For example, if you wanted to call the U.S. consulate in Acapulco, the whole number would be 011-52-744-469-0556. If you wanted to dial the U.S. embassy in Mexico City, the whole number would be 011-52-55-5209-9100.

To make international calls: To make international calls from Mexico, first dial 00, then the country code (U.S. or Canada 1, U.K. 44, Ireland 353, Australia 61, New Zealand 64). Next, dial the area code and number. For example, to call the British Embassy in Washington, you would dial 00-1-202-588-7800.

For directory assistance: Dial ✆ **040** if you're looking for a number inside Mexico. ***Note:*** Listings usually appear under the owner's name, not the name of the business, and your chances to find an English-speaking operator are slim to none.

For operator assistance: If you need operator assistance in making a call, dial 090 to make an international call, and 020 to call a number in Mexico.

Toll-free numbers: Numbers beginning with 800 within Mexico are toll-free, but calling a U.S. toll-free number from Mexico costs the same as an overseas call. To call an 800 number in the U.S., dial 001-880 and the last seven digits of the toll-free number. To call an 888 number in the U.S., dial 001-881 and the last seven digits of the toll-free number. For a number with an 887 prefix, dial 882; for 866, dial 883.

Time Zone Central Time prevails throughout most of Mexico, and for all of the areas covered in this book. Mexico observes **daylight saving time.**

Tipping Most service employees in Mexico count on tips for the majority of their income—that's especially true for bellboys and waiters. Bellboys should receive the equivalent of 50¢ to $1 per bag; waiters generally receive 10% to 20%, depending on the level of service. In Mexico, it is not customary to tip taxi drivers, unless they are hired by the hour or provide touring or other special services.

Useful Phone Numbers **Tourist Help Line,** available 24 hours (✆ 01-800/903-9200 toll-free inside Mexico). **Mexico Hotline** (✆ 800/44-MEXICO). **U.S. Dept. of State Travel Advisory,** staffed 24 hours (✆ 202/647-5225). **U.S. Passport Agency** (✆ 202/647-0518). **U.S. Centers for Disease Control International Traveler's Hotline** (✆ 404/332-4559).

Water Most hotels have decanters or bottles of purified water in the rooms, and the better hotels have either purified water from regular taps or special taps marked *agua purificada.* Some hotels charge for in-room bottled water. Virtually any hotel, restaurant, or bar will bring you purified water if you specifically request it, but you'll usually be charged for it. Bottled purified water is sold widely at drugstores and grocery stores. Some popular brands are **Santa Maria, Ciel, Agua Pura,** and **Pureza. Evian** and **Bonafont** are widely available.

2 Settling into Cancún

Mexico's calling card to the world, Cancún perfectly showcases both the country's breathtaking natural beauty and the depth of its 1,000-year history. Simply stated, Cancún is the reason most people travel to Mexico. The sheer number of travelers underscores Cancún's magnetic appeal, with almost three million people visiting this enticing beach resort annually—most of them on their first trip to the country. The reasons for this are both numerous and obvious.

Cancún offers an unrivaled combination of high-quality accommodations, dreamy beaches, easy air access, and a wide diversity of shopping, dining, nightlife, and nearby activities—most of them exceptional values. There is also the lure of ancient cultures evident in all directions and a number of ecologically oriented theme parks.

No doubt about it—Cancún embodies Caribbean splendor, with translucent turquoise waters and powdery white-sand beaches, coupled with coastal areas of great natural beauty. But Cancún is also a modern megaresort. Even a traveler apprehensive about visiting foreign soil will feel completely at ease here. English is spoken, dollars are accepted, roads are well paved, and lawns are manicured. Malls are the mode for shopping and dining, and you could swear that some hotels are larger than a small town. You do not need to spend a day getting your bearings, because you immediately see familiar names for dining, shopping, nightclubbing, and sleeping.

You may have heard that in 1974 a team of Mexican government computer analysts picked Cancún for tourism development for its ideal mix of elements to attract travelers—and they were right on. It's actually an island, a 24km (14-mile) sliver of land connected to the mainland by two bridges and separated from it by the expansive Nichupté lagoon. (*Cancún* means "golden snake" in Mayan.)

Cancún's luxury hotels have pools so spectacular that you may find it tempting to remain poolside, but don't. Set aside some time to simply gaze into the ocean and wriggle your toes in the fine, brilliantly white sand. It is, after all, what put Cancún on the map.

1 Orientation

GETTING THERE

BY PLANE **Aeromexico** (✆ **800/237-6639** in the U.S., or 01/800-021-4000 in Mexico; www.aeromexico.com) offers direct service from Atlanta, Houston, Miami, and New York, plus connecting service via Mexico City from Dallas, Los Angeles, and San Diego. **Mexicana** (✆ **800/531-7921** in the U.S., or 01/800-502-2000 or 998/881-9090 in Mexico; www.mexicana.com.mx) flies from Chicago, Denver, Los Angeles, Oakland, San Antonio, San Francisco, and San Jose via Mexico City, with nonstop service from Miami and New York. In addition to these carriers, many **charter** companies—such as Apple Vacations, Funjet, and Friendly Holidays—travel to Cancún; these package tours make up as much as 60% of arrivals by U.S. visitors (see "Packages for the Independent Traveler," in chapter 1).

Regional carrier **AeroCaribe,** a Mexicana affiliate (✆ **998/884-2000**) flies from Cozumel, Havana, Mexico City, Mérida, Chetumal, and other points within Mexico. You'll want to confirm departure times for flights to the U.S.; here are the Cancún airport numbers of major international carriers: **American** (✆ **998/883-4461;** www.aa.com), **Continental** (✆ **998/886-0006;** www.continental.com), and **Northwest** (✆ **998/886-0044** or 998/886-0046; www.nwa.com).

Most major car-rental firms have outlets at the airport, so if you're renting a car, consider picking it up and dropping it off at the airport to save on airport-transportation costs. Another way to save money is to arrange for the rental before you leave home. If you wait until you arrive, the daily cost will be around $50 to $75 for a Chevrolet Chevy or Athos. Major agencies include **Avis** (✆ **800/331-1212** in the U.S., or 998/886-0221; www.avis.com); **Budget** (✆ **800/527-0700** in the U.S., or 998/886-0417; fax 998/884-4812; www.budget.com); **Dollar** (✆ **800/800-4000** in the U.S., or 998/886-2300; www.dollar.com); **National** (✆ **800/328-4567** in the U.S., or 998/886-0655; www.nationalcar.com); and **Hertz** (✆ **800/654-3131** in the U.S. and Canada, or 998/884-1326; www.hertz.com). The Zona Hotelera (Hotel Zone) is 10km (6½ miles), or about a 20-minute drive, from the airport along wide, well-paved roads.

Rates for a private taxi from the airport are around $20 to downtown Cancún, or $28 to $40 to the Hotel Zone, depending on your destination. *Colectivos* (vans) run from the airport into town. Buy tickets, which cost about $9, from the booth to the far right as you exit the airport terminal. There's minibus transportation ($9.50) from the airport to the Puerto Juárez passenger ferry to Isla Mujeres, or you can hire a private taxi for about $40. There is no *colectivo* service returning to the airport from Ciudad Cancún or the Hotel Zone, so you'll have to take a taxi, but the rate will be much less than for the trip from the airport. (Only federally chartered taxis may take fares *from* the airport, but any taxi may bring passengers *to* the airport.) Ask at your hotel what the fare should be, but expect to pay about half what you paid from the airport to your hotel.

BY CAR From Mérida or Campeche, take Highway 180 east to Cancún. This is mostly a winding, two-lane road that branches off into the express toll road 180D between Izamal and Nuevo Xcan. Nuevo Xcan is approximately 42km (26 miles) from Cancún. Mérida is about 83km (52 miles) away, a 3½-hour drive.

BY BUS Cancún's **ADO bus terminal** (✆ **998/884-4352** or 998/884-4804) is in downtown Ciudad Cancún at the intersection of avenidas Tulum and Uxmal. All out-of-town buses arrive here. Buses run to Playa del Carmen, Tulum, Chichén Itzá, other nearby beach and archaeological zones, and other points within Mexico. For details on some popular destinations, see chapter 4, "Day Trips: Island Getaways & Nature Parks."

VISITOR INFORMATION

The **State Tourism Office,** Av. Tulum 26 (✆ **998/881-9000** or 998/884-8073), is centrally located downtown next to Banco Bancomer, immediately left of the Ayuntamiento Benito Juárez building, between avenidas Cobá and Uxmal. It's open Monday to Friday from 9am to 5pm. The **Convention & Visitors Bureau** tourist information office, Avenida Cobá at Avenida Tulum (✆ **998/884-6531** or 998/884-3438), next to Pizza Rolandi, is open Monday through Friday from 9am to 7pm. Each office lists hotels and their rates, and ferry schedules. For information prior to your arrival in Cancún, visit the Convention Bureau's website, **www.cancun.info**.

Pick up copies of the free monthly ***Cancún Tips*** booklet and a seasonal tabloid of the same name. The publications are owned by the same people who own the Captain's Cove restaurants, a couple of sightseeing boats, and timeshare hotels, so the information, though good, is not completely unbiased.

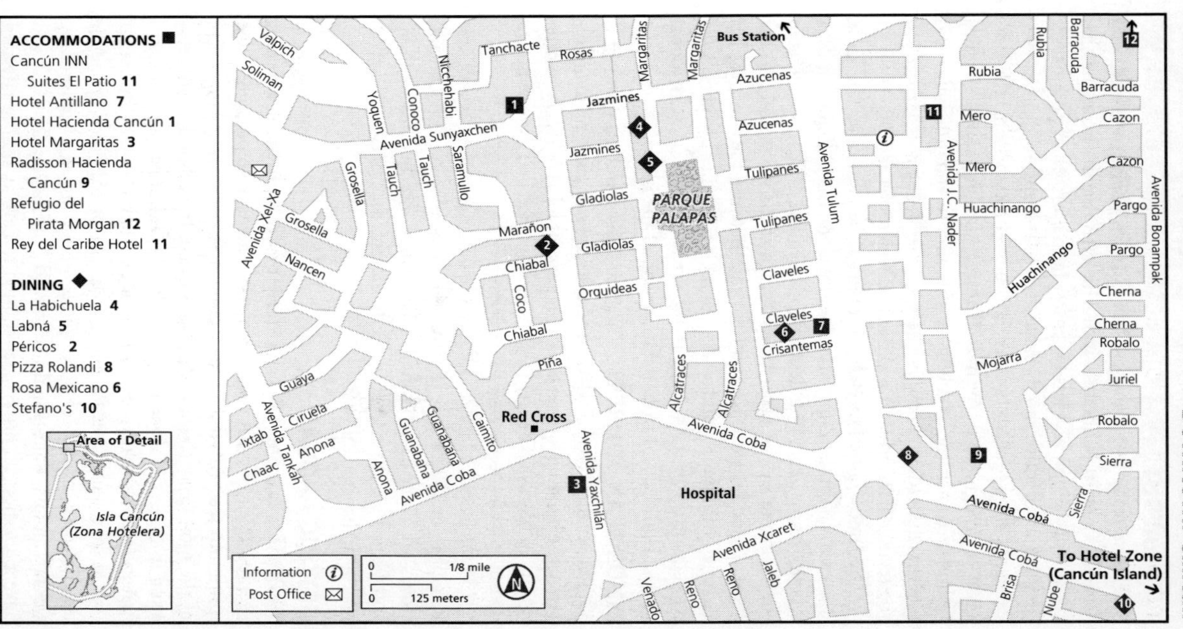

ACCOMMODATIONS ■
Cancún INN
Suites El Patio 11
Hotel Antillano 7
Hotel Hacienda Cancún 1
Hotel Margaritas 3
Radisson Hacienda
Cancún 9
Refugio del
Pirata Morgan 12
Rey del Caribe Hotel 11
DINING ◆
La Habichuela 4
Labná 5
Péricos 2
Pizza Rolandi 8
Rosa Mexicano 6
Stefano's 10
Area of Detail
Isla Cancún (Zona Hotelera)
Information
Post Office
0
1/8 mile
0
125 meters
N
To Hotel Zone (Cancún Island)
Bus Station
Hospital
Red Cross
PARQUE PALAPAS
Avenida Bonampak
Avenida J.C. Nader
Avenida Tulum
Avenida Yaxchilán
Avenida Sunyaxchen
Avenida Cobá
Avenida Coba
Avenida Xcaret
Avenida Tankah
Avenida Xel-Xa
Barracuda
Rubia
Mero
Huachinango
Cazon
Pargo
Cherna
Robalo
Juriel
Sierra
Mojarra
Nube
Brisa
Azucenas
Tulipanes
Claveles
Crisantemas
Alcatraces
Margaritas
Jazmines
Gladiolas
Orquideas
Rosas
Tanchacte
Nicchehabi
Conoco
Yoquen
Saramullo
Tauch
Grosella
Marañon
Chiabal
Coco
Piña
Caimito
Guanabana
Anona
Ciruela
Guaya
Nancen
Valpich
Soliman
Ixtab
Chaac
Jaleb
Reno
Venado

CITY LAYOUT

There are really two Cancúns: **Isla Cancún (Cancún Island)** and **Ciudad Cancún (Cancún City).** The latter, on the mainland, has restaurants, shops, and less-expensive hotels, as well as pharmacies, dentists, automotive shops, banks, travel and airline agencies, and car-rental firms—all within an area about 9 blocks square. The city's main thoroughfare is **Avenida Tulum.** Heading south, Avenida Tulum becomes the highway to the airport and to Tulum and Chetumal; heading north, it intersects the highway to Mérida and the road to Puerto Juárez and the Isla Mujeres ferries.

The famed **Zona Hotelera,** or Hotel Zone (also called the Zona Turística, or Tourist Zone) stretches out along Isla Cancún, which is a sandy strip 22km (14 miles) long, shaped like a "7." It connects to the mainland by the Playa Linda Bridge at the north end and the Punta Nizuc Bridge at the southern end. Between the two areas lies Laguna Nichupté. Avenida Cobá from Cancún City becomes Paseo Kukulkán, the island's main traffic artery. Cancún's international airport is just inland from the south end of the island.

FINDING AN ADDRESS Cancún's street-numbering system is a holdover from its early days. Addresses are still given by the number of the building lot and by the *manzana* (block) or *supermanzana* (group of blocks). The city is relatively compact, and the downtown commercial section is easy to cover on foot.

On the island, addresses are given by kilometer number on Paseo Kukulkán or by reference to some well-known location. In Cancún, streets are named after famous Maya cities. Chichén Itzá, Tulum, and Uxmal are the names of the boulevards in Cancún, as well as nearby archaeological sites.

GETTING AROUND

BY TAXI Taxi prices in Cancún are clearly set by zone, although keeping track of what's in which zone can take some doing. The minimum fare within the Hotel Zone is $5 per ride, making it one of the most expensive taxi areas in Mexico. In addition, taxis operating in the Hotel Zone feel perfectly justified in having a discriminatory pricing structure: Local residents pay about half of what tourists pay, and prices for guests at higher-priced hotels are about double those for budget hotel guests—these are all established by the taxi union. Rates should be posted outside your hotel; if you have a question, all drivers are required to have an official rate card in their taxis, though it's generally in Spanish.

Within the downtown area, the cost is about $1.50 per cab ride (not per person); within any other zone, it's $5. Traveling between two zones will also cost $5, and if you cross two zones, that'll cost $7.50. Settle on a price in advance, or check at your hotel. Trips to the airport from most zones cost $14. Taxis can also be rented for $18 per hour for travel around the city and Hotel Zone, but this rate can generally be negotiated down to $12 or less. If you want to hire a taxi to take you to Chichén Itzá or along the Riviera Maya, expect to pay about $30 per hour—many taxi drivers feel that they are also providing guide services.

BY BUS Bus travel within Cancún continues to improve and is increasingly popular. In town, almost everything is within walking distance. Ruta 1 and Ruta 2 (HOTELES) city buses travel frequently from the mainland to the beaches along Avenida Tulum (the main street) and all the way to Punta Nizuc at the far end of the Hotel Zone on Isla Cancún. Ruta 8 buses go to Puerto Juárez/Punta Sam for ferries to Isla Mujeres. They stop on the east side of Avenida Tulum. All these city buses operate between 6am and 10pm daily. Beware of private buses along the same route; they charge far more than the public ones. Public buses have the fare painted on the front; at press time, the fare was 60¢.

BY MOPED Mopeds are a convenient but dangerous way to cruise around through the very congested traffic. Rentals start at $25 for a day, and a credit card voucher is required as security. You should receive a crash helmet (it's the law) and instructions on how to lock the wheels when you park. Read the fine print on the back of the rental agreement regarding liability for repairs or replacement in case of accident, theft, or vandalism.

FAST FACTS: Cancún

American Express The local office is at Av. Tulum 208 and Agua (✆ **998/881-4000** or 998/881-4055; www.americanexpress.com/mexico), 1 block past the Plaza México. It's open Monday through Friday from 9am to 6pm, Saturday from 9am to 1pm. Another branch of American Express is located in the hotel zone, in the La Isla Shopping Center (✆ **998/885-3905**).

Area Code The telephone area code is **998**.

Climate It's hot but not overwhelmingly humid. The rainy season is May through October. August through October is hurricane season, which brings erratic weather. November through February is generally sunny but can also be cloudy, windy, somewhat rainy, and even cool.

Consulates The **U.S. Consular Agent** is in the Plaza Caracol 2, Paseo Kukulkán Km 8.5, third level, 320–323 (✆ **998/883-0272**). The office is open Monday through Friday from 9am to 1pm. The **Canadian Consulate** is in the Plaza México 312 (✆ **998/883-3360**). The office is open Monday through Friday from 9am to 5pm. The **United Kingdom** has a consular office in Cancún (✆ **998/881-0100,** ext. 65898; fax 998/848-8662; information@britishconsulatecancun.com). Irish, Australian, and New Zealand citizens should contact their embassies in Mexico City.

Crime Car break-ins are just about the only crime here. They happen frequently, especially around the shopping centers in the Hotel Zone. VW Beetles and Golfs are frequent targets.

Currency Exchange Most banks are downtown along Avenida Tulum and are usually open Monday through Friday from 9:30am to 5pm. Many have automated teller machines for after-hours cash withdrawals. In the Hotel Zone, you'll find banks in the Plaza Kukulcan and next to the convention center. There are also many *casas de cambio* (exchange houses). Downtown merchants are eager to change cash dollars, but island stores don't offer very good exchange rates. Avoid changing money at the airport as you arrive, especially at the first exchange booth you see—its rates are less favorable than those of any in town or others farther inside the airport concourse.

Drugstores With locations in both Flamingo Plaza (✆ **998/885-1351**) and Plaza Kukulcan (✆ **998/885-0860**), **Farmacia Roxana's** offers delivery service within the Hotel Zone. Plenty of drugstores are in the major shopping malls in the Hotel Zone, and are open until 10pm. In downtown Cancún, **Farmacia Cancún** is located at Avenida Tulum (✆ **998/884-1283**). You can stock up on Retin-A, Viagra, and many other prescription drugs without a prescription.

Emergencies To report an emergency, dial ✆ **060.** For first aid, the **Cruz Roja,** or Red Cross (✆ **065** or **998/884-1616;** fax 998/883-9218), is open 24 hours on Avenida Yaxchilán between avenidas Xcaret and Labná, next to the Telmex building. **Total Assist,** Claveles 5, SM 22, at Avenida Tulum (✆ **998/884-1058** or 998/884-1092; totalassist@prodigy.net.mx), is a small (nine-room) emergency hospital with English-speaking doctors. It's open 24 hours and accepts American Express, MasterCard, and Visa. Desk staff may have limited command of English. Another facility that caters to English-speaking visitors is **Ameri-Med** (Plaza Las Americas, in downtown Cancún; ✆ **998/881-3434**) with 24-hour emergency service. Air Ambulance service is available by calling ✆ **01-800/305-9400** in Mexico.

Internet Access **C@ncunet,** in a kiosk on the second floor of Plaza Kukulcan, Paseo Kukulkán Km 13 (✆ **998/885-0880**), offers Internet access at $2 for 10 minutes, or $7 per hour. It's open daily from 10am to 10pm.

Luggage Storage & Lockers Hotels will generally tag and store luggage while you travel elsewhere.

Newspapers & Magazines Most hotel gift shops and newsstands carry English-language magazines and English-language Mexican newspapers.

Police Cancún has a fleet of English-speaking tourist police to help travelers. Dial ✆ **998/884-1913** or 998/884-2342. The ***Procuraduría Federal del Consumidor*** (consumer protection agency), Av. Cobá 9–11 (✆ **998/884-2634** or 998/884-2701), is opposite the Social Security Hospital and upstairs from the Fenix drugstore. It's open Monday through Saturday from 9am to 3pm.

Post Office The main *correo* is at the intersection of avenidas Sunyaxchen and Xel-Ha (✆ **998/884-1418**). It's open Monday through Friday from 9am to 4pm, and Saturday from 9am to noon just for the purchase of stamps.

Safety Aside from car break-ins, there is very little crime in Cancún. People are generally safe late at night in tourist areas; just use ordinary common sense. As at any other beach resort, don't take money or valuables to the beach. See "Crime," above.

Swimming on the Caribbean side presents a danger because of the undertow. See the information on beaches in chapter 3, "Beaches, Watersports & Boat Tours," for information about flag warnings

Seasons Technically, high season is from December 15 to April; low season is from May to December 15, when prices drop 10% to 30%. Some hotels are starting to charge high-season rates during June and July, when Mexican, European, and school-holiday visitors often travel, although rates may still be lower than in winter months.

Special Events See the "Cancún Calendar of Festivals & Special Events" in chapter 1.

2 Where to Stay

Island hotels—almost all of them offering clean, modern facilities—line the beach like dominoes. Extravagance is the byword in the newer hotels. Some hotels, while exclusive, affect a more relaxed attitude. The water on the upper end of the island facing Bahía de Mujeres is placid, while beaches lining the long side of the island facing the Caribbean are subject to choppier water and crashing waves on windy days. (For more information on swimming safety, see "Beaches, Watersports & Boat Tours," in chapter 3.) Be aware that the farther south you go on the island, the longer it takes (20–30 min. in traffic) to get back to the "action spots," which are primarily between the Plaza Flamingo and Punta Cancún on the island and along Avenida Tulum on the mainland.

Almost all major hotel chains are represented on Cancún Island, so this list can be viewed as a representative summary, with a select number of notable places. The reality is that Cancún is so popular as a package destination from the U.S. that prices and special deals are often the deciding factor for those traveling here (see "Packages for the Independent Traveler," in chapter 1). Ciudad Cancún offers independently owned, smaller, less expensive lodging; prices are lower here off season (May to early Dec). For condo, home, and villa rentals, check with **Cancún Hideaways** (www.cancun-hideaways.com), a company specializing in luxury properties, downtown apartments, and condos—many at prices much lower than comparable hotel stays. Owner Maggie Rodriguez, a former resident of Cancún, has made this niche market her specialty.

The hotel listings in this chapter begin on Cancún Island and finish in Cancún City, where bargain lodgings are available. Parking is free at all island hotels.

Isla Cancún (Zona Hotelera)

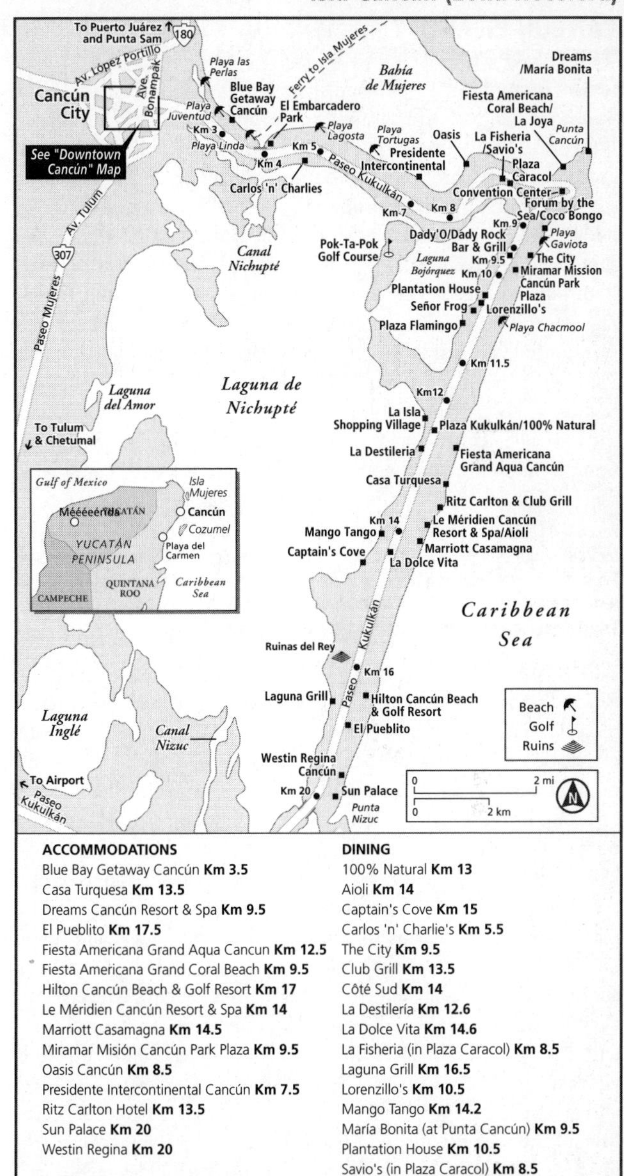

ACCOMMODATIONS

Blue Bay Getaway Cancún **Km 3.5**
Casa Turquesa **Km 13.5**
Dreams Cancún Resort & Spa **Km 9.5**
El Pueblito **Km 17.5**
Fiesta Americana Grand Aqua Cancun **Km 12.5**
Fiesta Americana Grand Coral Beach **Km 9.5**
Hilton Cancún Beach & Golf Resort **Km 17**
Le Méridien Cancún Resort & Spa **Km 14**
Marriott Casamagna **Km 14.5**
Miramar Misión Cancún Park Plaza **Km 9.5**
Oasis Cancún **Km 8.5**
Presidente Intercontinental Cancún **Km 7.5**
Ritz Carlton Hotel **Km 13.5**
Sun Palace **Km 20**
Westin Regina **Km 20**

DINING

100% Natural **Km 13**
Aioli **Km 14**
Captain's Cove **Km 15**
Carlos 'n' Charlie's **Km 5.5**
The City **Km 9.5**
Club Grill **Km 13.5**
Côté Sud **Km 14**
La Destilería **Km 12.6**
La Dolce Vita **Km 14.6**
La Fisheria (in Plaza Caracol) **Km 8.5**
Laguna Grill **Km 16.5**
Lorenzillo's **Km 10.5**
Mango Tango **Km 14.2**
María Bonita (at Punta Cancún) **Km 9.5**
Plantation House **Km 10.5**
Savio's (in Plaza Caracol) **Km 8.5**

CANCUN ISLAND

VERY EXPENSIVE

Casa Turquesa ★ Romantic, tranquil, and elegant, Casa Turquesa is an oasis of relaxation in the midst of this playful island. If the Mediterranean-style ambience weren't appealing enough, their exceptional stretch of beach (fronting brilliant turquoise waters) is sure to inspire a positive attitude adjustment. This is a true boutique hotel catering to couples and noted for its exceptional service. All suites feature queen- or king-size beds, plus balconies with Jacuzzis. Bathrooms themselves are extra large, with double sinks and a separate tub and shower. Blue-and-white canopy shade tents dot the area surrounding the attractive pool and beach; the adjacent Turquesa Pool Bar is open from 10am to 5pm daily. For dining, the Belle-Vue restaurant, serving international gourmet fare, is open 24 hours, and the formal Celebrity restaurant serves seafood and Angus beef from 6pm to midnight. For those who prefer not to leave the comfort of their room, 24-hour room service is also available.

Paseo Kukulkán, Km 13.5, 77500 Cancún, Q. Roo. ✆ **888/528-8300** in the U.S., or 998/885-2925. Fax 998/885-2922. www.casaturquesa.com. 33 suites. High season $204–$231; low season $136–$145. AE, DC, MC, V. Free parking. **Amenities:** 2 restaurants; 2 bars; pool; 24-hr. room service; concierge; travel agency. *In room:* A/C, TV, minibar, hair dryer, iron, safe, CD player, bathrobes.

Fiesta Americana Grand Aqua Cancun ★★★ Stunning, stylish, and sensual, Aqua is certain to emerge as Cancún's most coveted place to stay. A new member of the Fiesta Americana chain, the resort was on the brink of opening at press time, so I can't comment on service or the actual details of a stay, but I was so enthused at its opening, I couldn't wait to share the news. The entire hotel seems to mirror the predominant colors of Cancún—turquoise and white—in a sublimely chic manner. This hotel was built for sophisticated travelers who appreciate hip style and look for the cutting edge in places to stay. Aqua aims to stimulate your five senses, and upon arrival—under a crystal cube fountain—you're offered a fusion tea, and a blend of relaxing and stimulating aromatherapy. The oasis of eight oceanfront pools is surrounded by chaises, queen-size recliners, and private cabanas. All rooms and common areas emphasize the views to the pool and ocean beyond. Rooms are generous in size, and all face the ocean and have balconies. Very large bathrooms feature a large soaking tub and organic bath products. Guests can tailor their turndown service by selecting from a pillow menu and choice of aromatherapy oils and candles. Miniature Zen gardens or a fishbowl add unique touches to room decor. Suites offer extras like Boise surround-sound systems. Twenty-nine rooms are "Grand Club," which includes continental breakfast and a club room with butler service, snacks, bar service, and private check-in. The 1,500-sq.-m (500-sq.-ft.) spa is among the hotel's most notable attractions, with 12 treatment rooms offering a blend of Eastern, pre-Hispanic, and Western treatments. Outdoor Pilates, Tai Chi, and yoga classes are offered daily, and massage cabanas are also available on the beach. Another hallmark of this hotel is certain to be its collection of restaurants, chief among them **SIETE,** under the direction of premier Mexican chef and cookbook author Patricia Quintana, featuring her sophisticated take on traditional Mexican cuisine. Chef Michelle Bernstein, formerly a rising culinary star in Miami, presides over **MB,** serving healthy comfort food. There's also an Italian restaurant, deli, lounge, and 24-hour room service. After dark, the hotel shifts moods, with fire pits, torchlight, and ambient music.

Paseo Kukulkán Km 12.5, 77500 Cancún, Q. Roo. ✆ **800/FIESTA-1** in the U.S., or 998/881-7600. Fax 998/881-7601. www.fiestaamericana.com. 371 units. High season $393–$466 double, $516 Grand Club double, $750 suite; low season $215–$313 double, $363 Grand Club double, $600 suite. Ask about Fiesta Break packages. AE, DC, MC, V. Free parking. Small pets allowed with prior reservation. **Amenities:** 4 restaurants; lounge and bar; poolside snack bar; 8 swimming pools; tennis court; fitness center and spa w/12 treatment rooms; watersports on the beach; concierge; travel agency; business center; salon; room service; babysitting; laundry service; Club floors w/special amenities and complimentary cocktails. *In room:* A/C, flatscreen TV and DVD, high-speed Internet access, minibar, hair dryer, iron, safe, CD player.

Fiesta Americana Grand Coral Beach ★ This is an ideal choice for any type of traveler looking to be at the heart of all that Cancún has to offer. The spectacular hotel, which opened in 1991, has one of the best locations in Cancún, with 300m (1,000 ft.) of prime beachfront and proximity to the main shopping and entertainment centers. The key word here is *big*—everything at the Fiesta Americana seems oversize, from the lobby to the suites. Service is gracious, if cool: The hotel aims for a sophisticated ambience. It's embellished with elegant dark-green granite and an abundance of marble. The large guest rooms are also decorated with marble, and all have balconies facing the ocean, most of which were remodeled in 2004. The hotel's great Punta Cancún location (opposite the convention center) has the advantage of facing the beach to the north, meaning that the surf is calm and perfect for swimming.

Paseo Kukulkán Km 9.5, 77500 Cancún, Q. Roo. ✆ **800/343-7821** in the U.S., or 998/881-3200. Fax 998/881-3273. www.fiestamericana.com. 602 units. High season $328–$555 double, $529–$650 Club Floor double, $875 Caribbean suite; low season $222–$424 double, $381–$504 Club Floor double, $695 Caribbean suite. AE, MC, V. **Amenities:** 3 restaurants (including the gourmet Basilique); 5 bars; swimming pool w/swim-up bars; poolside snack bar; 3 indoor tennis courts w/stadium seating; fitness center w/weights, sauna, and massage; watersports rentals on the beach; concierge; travel agency; car rental; business center; salon; room service; babysitting; laundry service; 2 concierge floors w/complimentary cocktails; 2 junior suites for travelers w/disabilities are available. *In room:* A/C, TV, minibar, hair dryer, iron, safe.

Hilton Cancún Beach & Golf Resort ★ *Kids* Grand, expansive, and fully equipped, this is a true resort in every sense of the word and is especially perfect for anyone whose motto is "the bigger the better." The Hilton Cancún, sits on 100 hectares (250 acres) of prime beachside property, a location that gives every room a sea view (some have both sea and lagoon views), with an 18-hole par-72 golf course across the street. Like the sprawling resort, rooms are grandly spacious and immaculately decorated in minimalist style, all of which were renovated in 2004. Area rugs and pale furnishings soften marble floors and bathrooms throughout. It's a very "kid-friendly" hotel, with one of the island's best children's activity programs, special children's pool, and babysitting available. The hotel is especially appealing to golfers because it's one of only two in Cancún with an on-site course (the other is the Meliá). Greens fees for guests are $77 for 9 holes, $99 for 18 holes, and include the use of a cart. Just opened is the new Wellness Spa, highlights of which are oceanfront massage cabanas, yoga, and aromatherapy.

Paseo Kukulkán Km 17, Retorno Lacandones, 77500 Cancún, Q. Roo. ✆ **800/228-3000** in the U.S., or 998/881-8000. Fax 998/881-8080. www.hiltoncancun.com.mx. 426 units. High season $269–$415 double, $440–$585 Beach Club double, $555–$779 suite; low season $119–$300 double, $350–$550 Beach Club double, $395–$500 suite. AE, DC, MC, V. **Amenities:** 2 restaurants; 7 interconnected pools w/swim-up bar; golf course across the street; 2 lighted tennis courts; Wellness Spa w/spa services and fully equipped gym; 2 whirlpools; watersports center; Kids Club; concierge; tour desk; car rental; salon; room service; babysitting; laundry service; golf clinic. *In room:* A/C, TV, minibar, coffeemaker, hair dryer, iron, safe, bathrobes, house shoes.

Le Méridien Cancún Resort & Spa ★★★ Of all the luxury properties in Cancún, Le Méridien is the most inviting, with a refined yet welcoming sense of personal service. From the intimate lobby and reception area to the best concierge service in Cancún, guests feel immediately pampered. The relatively small establishment is more elegant boutique hotel than immense resort—a welcome

Tips An Important Note on Hotel Prices

Cancún's hotels, in all price categories, generally set their rates in dollars, so they are immune to swings in the peso. Travel agents and wholesalers always have air/hotel packages available, and Sunday papers often advertise inventory-clearing packages at prices much lower than the rates listed here. Cancún also has numerous all-inclusive properties, which allow you to take a fixed-cost vacation. Note that the price quoted when you call a hotel's reservation number from the United States may not include Cancún's 12% tax. Prices can vary considerably throughout the year, so it pays to consult a travel agent or shop around.

relief. The decor throughout the rooms and common areas is classy and comforting, not overdone. Rooms are generous in size, and most have small balconies overlooking the pool, with a view to the ocean. Each has a very large marble bathroom with a separate tub and glassed-in shower. The hotel attracts many Europeans as well as younger, sophisticated travelers, and is ideal for a second honeymoon or romantic break.

A highlight of—or even a reason for—staying here is the **Spa del Mar,** one of Mexico's most complete European spa facilities, with more than 4,570 sq. m (15,000 sq. ft.) of services dedicated to your body and soul. A complete fitness center with extensive cardio and weight machines is on the upper level. The spa consists of a health snack bar, a full-service salon, and 14 treatment rooms, as well as men's and women's steam rooms, saunas, whirlpools, cold plunge pool, inhalation rooms, tranquillity rooms, lockers, and changing areas.

Retorno del Rey Km 14, Zona Hotelera, 77500, Cancún, Q. Roo. ✆ **800/543-4300** in the U.S., or 998/881-2200. Fax 998/881-2201. www.lemeridien.com. 213 units. High season $290 double, $450 suite; low season $220 double, $350 suite. Ask about special spa packages. Additional $10 per day resort fee enables access to Spa de Mar, kids' club, and other extra services. AE, DC, MC, V. Small pets accepted with prior reservation. **Amenities:** 2 restaurants (including Aioli; see "Where to Dine," later in this chapter); lobby bar; 3 cascading swimming pools; 2 lighted championship tennis courts; whirlpool; watersports equipment and massage *palapa* on the beach; supervised children's program w/clubhouse, play equipment, wading pool; concierge; tour desk; car rental; business center w/Internet access; small shopping arcade; 24-hr. room service; babysitting; laundry service. *In room:* A/C, TV, dataport, minibar, hair dryer, iron, safe.

Ritz-Carlton Hotel ★★★ For those who want to feel indulged, this is the place to stay. On 3 hectares (7½ acres), the nine-story Ritz-Carlton sets the standard for elegance in Cancún. The hotel fronts a 370m (1,200-ft.) white-sand beach, and all rooms overlook the ocean, pool, and tropical gardens. The style—in both public areas and guest rooms—is sumptuous and formal, with thick carpets, elaborate chandeliers, and fresh flowers throughout. In all rooms, marble bathrooms have telephones, separate tubs and showers, and lighted makeup mirrors. The recently opened Kayantá Spa offers an excellent selection of Mayan and Mexican-inspired treatments and massages. The hotel has won countless accolades for service.

Retorno del Rey 36, off Paseo Kukulkán Km 13.5, 77500 Cancún, Q. Roo. ✆ **800/241-3333** in the U.S. and Canada, or 998/881-0808. Fax 998/881-0815. www.ritzcarlton.com. 365 units. High season $369–$475 double, $389–$850 Club floor and suites; low season $189–$279 double, $295–$429 Club floor and suites. Ask about golf, spa, and weekend packages. AE, MC, V. **Amenities:** 5 restaurants (including the Club Grill, one of the best restaurants in the city; see "Where to Dine," later in this chapter); Lobby Lounge (see "Cancun After Dark," in chapter 3); 2 connecting swimming pools (heated in winter); 3 lighted tennis courts; fully equipped fitness center and Kayantá Spa; Ritz Kids program w/supervised activities; concierge; travel agency; business center; shopping arcade; salon; 24-hr. room service; babysitting; laundry service; dry cleaning; Club floors; deluxe beach cabañas for 2. *In room:* A/C, TV, dataport, minibar, hair dryer, iron, safe, bathrobes.

Riu Palace Las Américas ★★ The all-inclusive Riu Palace is part of a family of Riu resorts in Cancún known for their grand, opulent style. This one is the smallest of the three in Cancún, and the most elegant, steeped in pearl-white Greco style, and my choice for a high-end all-inclusive vacation in Cancún. The location is prime—near the central shopping, dining, and nightlife centers, just 5 minutes walking to the Convention Center. All rooms are spacious junior suites with ocean or lagoon views, a separate seating area, and a balcony or terrace. Eight also feature a Jacuzzi. Two central pools overlook the ocean and a wide stretch of beach, with one heated during winter months. The hotel offers guests virtually 24 hours of all-inclusive snacks, meals, and beverages. And, if that's not enough, guests have exchange privileges at the Riu Cancún, next door.

Bulevar Kukulkán, Lote 4, 77500 Cancún, Q. Roo. ✆ **888/666-8816** in the U.S., or 998/891-4300. www.riu.com. 368 units. High season $413–$627 double; low season $287–$464 double. Rates are all-inclusive. AE, MC, V. Free, unguarded parking. **Amenities:** 6 restaurants; 5 bars; 2 pools; tennis; fitness center; spa (extra charges apply); solarium; sports program; windsurfing; room service. *In room:* A/C, TV, hair dryer, iron, safe, bathrobes.

Sun Palace ★ If you're looking for an all-inclusive resort on a great stretch of Caribbean beach, this member of the popular Palace Resorts chain is a prime pick—and the most elegant of the Palace properties in Cancún. The fantastic beach is one of the widest on the island. Located toward the southern end of the island, next to the Westin Regina, this all-suite resort is farther away from the action of the hotel zone—which may be what you want, considering all of the goodies that go with staying here. One of the best perks is that the activities program includes excursions to Tulum, Chichén Itzá, or Isla Mujeres. Suites feature modern Mexican decor, and all have marble floors and a combination bath with whirlpool tub. All units have oceanview balconies or terraces. In addition to the beachside pool, there's an indoor pool, plus a large Jacuzzi with a waterfall. A nicely equipped health club and tennis court complement the ample activities program. When you stay at a Palace resort, you have the option at playing at any of the other members of the chain—there are two in Cancún and three others farther south along the Riviera Maya.

Paseo Kukulkán Km 20, 77500 Cancún, Q. Roo. ✆ **800/346-8225** in the U.S., or 998/85-0533. Fax 998/885-1593. www.palaceresorts.com. 237 suites. High season $310–$398 suite; low season $270–$350 suite. Rates are all-inclusive. AE, DC, MC, V. **Amenities:** 3 restaurants; 2 pools (1 indoor); tennis court; health club; Jacuzzi; 24-hr. room service. *In room:* A/C, TV, hair dryer, iron, safe, bathrobes.

EXPENSIVE

Dreams Cancún Resort & Spa ★★ *Kids* Formerly the Camino Real Cancún, the all-inclusive Dreams Resort is among the island's most appealing places to stay, located on 1.5 hectares (4 acres) at the tip of Punta Cancún. The setting is sophisticated, but the hotel is very welcoming to children. The architecture of the hotel is contemporary and sleek, with bright colors and strategic angles. Rooms in the newer 18-story Club section have extra services and amenities; rates here include full breakfast. The lower-priced rooms have lagoon views. Dreams all-inclusive concept is more oriented to quality experiences than unlimited buffets—your room price here includes gourmet meals, 24-hour room service, premium brand drinks, as well as the use of all resort amenities, watersports, evening entertainment, airport transfers, and tips. The fitness center and spa are the focal points of the resort's amenities.

Paseo Kukulkán, 77500 Punta Cancún (Apdo. Postal 14), Cancún, Q. Roo. ✆ **866/237-3267** in the U.S., or 998/848-7000. Fax 998/848-7001. www.dreamscancun.com. 381 units. High season $275 double, $320 Club double; low season $195 double,

$230 Club double. AE, DC, MC, V. **Amenities:** 3 restaurants; nightclub; pool; private saltwater lagoon w/sea turtles and tropical fish; 3 lighted tennis courts; fitness center w/steam bath; watersports center; sailing pier; Jet Skis; beach volleyball; travel agency; car rental; 24-hour business center with Internet access salon; 24-hr. room service; massage; babysitting (w/advance notice). *In room:* A/C, TV, minibar, hair dryer, iron, safe.

Marriott Casa Magna ★★ Kids This is quintessential Marriott—those who are familiar with the chain's standards will feel at home here and appreciate the hotel's attention to detailed service. Entering through a half-circle of Roman columns, you pass through a domed foyer to a wide, lavishly marbled 14m-high (44-ft.) lobby filled with plants and shallow pools. Guest rooms hold contemporary furnishings, tiled floors, and ceiling fans; most have balconies. The hotel caters to family travelers with specially priced packages (up to two children stay free with parent) and the Club Amigos supervised children's program. In 2001 Marriott opened the 450-room luxury **JW Marriott Cancún,** Paseo Kukulkán Km 14.5, 77500 Cancún, Q. Roo (✆ **998/848-9600;** www.marriott.com), on the beach next to the Casa Magna.

Paseo Kukulkán Km 14.5, 77500 Cancún, Q. Roo ✆ **800/228-9290** in the U.S., or 998/881-2000. Fax 998/881-2085. www.marriott.com. 452 units. High season $225–$254 double, $350 suite; low season $139–$160 double, $300 suite. Ask about packages. AE, MC, V. **Amenities:** 5 restaurants; lobby bar w/live music; swimming pool; 2 lighted tennis courts; health club w/saunas, whirlpool, aerobics, and juice bar; concierge; travel agency; car rental; salon w/massage and facials; room service; babysitting; laundry service. *In room:* A/C, TV, dataport, minibar, coffeemaker, hair dryer, iron, safe.

Presidente Inter-Continental Cancún ★ On the island's best beach, facing the placid Bahía de Mujeres, the Presidente's location is reason enough to stay here, and it's just a 2-minute walk to Cancún's public Pok-Ta-Pok Golf Club (Club de Golf Cancún). For its ambience, I consider it an ideal choice for a romantic getaway or for couples who enjoy indulging in the sports of golf, tennis, or even shopping. Cool and spacious, the Presidente sports a postmodern design with lavish marble and wicker accents and a strong use of color. Guests have a choice of two double beds or one king. All rooms have tastefully simple unfinished pine furniture. Sixteen units on the first floor have patios with outdoor whirlpool tubs. The expansive pool has a pyramid-shaped waterfall. Coming from Cancún City, you'll reach the Presidente on the left side of the street before you get to Punta Cancún.

Paseo Kukulkán Km 7.5, 77500 Cancún, Q. Roo. ✆ **800/327-0200** in the U.S., or 998/848-8700. Fax 998/883-2602. www.interconti.com. 299 units. High season

$240–$300 double; low season $150–$230 double. Rates include unlimited golf at Pok-Ta-Pok. AE, MC, V. Ask about special packages. **Amenities:** 3 restaurants; 2 swimming pools; lighted tennis courts; fitness center; whirlpool; watersports equipment rental; travel agency; car rental; shopping arcade; 24-hr. room service; babysitting; laundry service; nonsmoking floors; Club floors; 2 rooms for travelers w/disabilities are available; marina. *In room:* A/C, TV, dataport, minibar, hair dryer, safe.

Westin Regina Cancún ★★ The strikingly austere architecture of the Westin Regina, impressive with its elegant use of stone and marble, is the stamp of leading Latin American architect Ricardo Legorreta. The hotel consists of two sections, the main building and the more exclusive six-story hot-pink tower. Standard rooms are unusually large and beautifully furnished with cool, contemporary furniture. Those on the sixth floor have balconies, and first-floor rooms have terraces. Rooms in the tower all have ocean or lagoon views, furniture with Olinalá lacquer accents, Berber area rugs, oak tables and chairs, and terraces with lounge chairs. It's important to note that this hotel is a 15- to 20-minute ride from the lively strip that lies between the Plaza Flamingo and Punta Cancún, so it's a good choice for those who want a little more seclusion than Cancún typically offers. However, it is easy to join the action—buses stop in front, and taxis are readily available.

Paseo Kukulkán Km 20, 77500 Cancún, Q. Roo. ✆ **800/228-3000** in the U.S., 01-800/215-7000 in Mexico, or 998/848-7400. Fax 998/885-0666. www.westin.com. 293 units. High season $285–$450 double; low season $160–$299 double. AE, DC, MC, V. **Amenities:** 2 restaurants; 2 bars; 5 swimming pools; 2 lighted tennis courts; gym w/Stairmaster, bicycle, weights, aerobics, sauna, steam, massage; *temazcal* (sweat lodge); 3 whirlpools; concierge; travel agency; car rental; salon; room service; babysitting; laundry service; pharmacy/gift shop. *In room:* A/C, TV, dataport, minibar, coffeemaker, hair dryer, iron, safe.

MODERATE

Blue Bay Getaway Cancún ★ The adults-only Blue Bay Getaway Cancún is a spirited yet relaxing all-inclusive resort favored by young adults. Surrounded by acres of tropical gardens, it's ideally located at the northern end of the Hotel Zone, close to the major shopping plazas, restaurants, and nightlife. It has a terrific beach with calm waters for swimming. The comfortable, modern rooms are in two sections. The central building features 72 rooms decorated in rustic wood, the main lobby, administrative offices, restaurants, and Las Margaritas bar. The remaining nine buildings feature colorful Mexican decor; rooms have lagoon, garden, and ocean views. Safes are available for an extra charge. During the evenings, guests may enjoy a variety of theme-night dinners, nightly shows, and live entertainment in an outdoor theater. Note that clothing is optional on the beaches of this Blue Bay resort.

Paseo Kukulkán Km 3.5, 77500 Cancún, Q. Roo. ✆ **800/211-1000** in the U.S., or 998/848-7900. Fax 998/848-7994. www.bluebayresorts.com. 385 units. High season $280 double; low season $180 double. Rates include food, beverages, and activities. AE, MC, V. **Amenities:** 4 restaurants; 4 bars; 3 swimming pools; tennis court; exercise room w/daily aerobics classes; 4 whirlpools; watersports equipment; snorkeling and scuba lessons; bicycles; game room w/pool and Ping-Pong tables; rooms for those w/limited mobility; marina. *In room:* A/C, TV, dataport, hair dryer.

El Pueblito ★ *Kids* This hotel offers perhaps the top all-inclusive value in Cancún. Dwarfed by its ostentatious neighbors, the El Pueblito lobby resembles a traditional Mexican hacienda, with several three-story buildings (no elevators) terraced in a V-shape down a gentle hillside toward the sea. A meandering swimming pool with waterfalls runs between the two series of buildings. Rooms are very large, with modern rattan furnishings, travertine marble floors, and large bathrooms. Each has either a balcony or a terrace. In addition to a constant flow of buffet-style meals and snacks, there's also the choice of a nightly theme party, complete with entertainment. Minigolf and a water slide, plus a full program of kids' activities, make this an ideal place for families with children. The hotel is located toward the southern end of the island past the Hilton Resort.

Paseo Kukulkán Km 17.5, 77500 Cancún, Q. Roo. ✆ **998/885-0422** or 998/881-8814. Fax 998/885-0731. www.pueblitohotels.com. 349 units. High season $300 double; low season $240 double. Rates are all-inclusive. Ask about specials. AE, MC, V. **Amenities:** 3 restaurants; lobby cafe; 2 bars; large pool; tennis courts; nonmotorized watersports; babysitting ($10 per hour); aerobics; volleyball; cooking classes. *In room:* A/C, TV.

Miramar Misión Cancún Park Plaza Each of the ingeniously designed rooms here has a partial view of both the lagoon and the ocean. Public spaces throughout the hotel have lots of dark wood accents, but the most notable feature is the large, rectangular swimming pool that extends through the hotel and down to the beach, with built-in, submerged sun chairs. There's also an oversize whirlpool (the largest in Cancún), a sun deck, and a snack bar on the seventh-floor roof. Rooms are on the small side but are bright and comfortable, with small balconies and bamboo furniture; bathrooms have polished limestone vanities. A popular nightclub, **Batacha,** has live music for dancing from 9pm to 4am Tuesday through Sunday.

Paseo Kukulkán Km 9.5, 77500 Zona Hotelera Cancún, Q. Roo. ✆ **800/215-1333** in the U.S., or 998/883-1755. Fax 998/883-1136. www.hotelesmision.com. 266 units. High season $220 double; low season $160 double. AE, MC, V. **Amenities:** 3 restaurants; 2 bars; rooftop snack bar; pool; whirlpool. *In room:* A/C, TV, minibar, hair dryer, safe.

Oasis Cancún From the street, this hotel may not be much to look at, but on the ocean side you'll find a small but pretty patio garden and Cancún's best beach for safe swimming. The location is ideal, close to all the shops and restaurants near Punta Cancún and the Convention Center. Rooms overlook the lagoon or the ocean, and all were remodeled in 2004. They are large, with pleasing, comfortable decor, marble floors, and either two double beds or a king-size bed.. Several studios have kitchenettes.

Paseo Kukulkán Km 8.5, 77500 Cancún, Q. Roo. ✆ **800/221-2222** in the U.S., or 998/883-0800. Fax 998/883-2087 units. High season $145–$250 double; low season $138–$158 double. Rates include buffet breakfast. Children under 12 stay free in parent's room. AE, MC, V. **Amenities:** Restaurant; 2 snack bars; 3 bars; 2 swimming pools (1 for adults, 1 for children); 2 lighted tennis courts; watersports equipment rental; nonsmoking areas; wheelchair access; marina. *In room:* A/C, TV.

CANCUN CITY

MODERATE

Radisson Hacienda Cancún ★★ *Value* This is the nicest hotel in downtown Cancún, and one of the best values in the area. The Radisson offers all the expected comforts of a chain, yet in an atmosphere of Mexican hospitality. Resembling a hacienda, rooms are set off from a large rotunda-style lobby, lush gardens, and a pleasant pool area. All have brightly colored fabric accents; views of the garden, the pool, or the street; and a small sitting area and balcony. Bathrooms have a combination tub and shower. Guests have access to a shuttle service to Isla Cancún's beaches, or to the Pok-Ta-Pok Golf course. The hotel is behind the state government building, within walking distance of downtown Cancún dining and shopping.

Av. Náder 1, SM2, Centro, 77500 Cancún, Q. Roo. ✆ **800/333-3333** in the U.S., or 998/887-4455. Fax 998/884-7954. www.radissoncancun.com. 248 units. High season $100 double, $125 junior suite; low season $90 double, $115 junior suite. Ask about special all-inclusive rates. AE, MC, V. **Amenities:** 2 restaurants; lively lobby bar; pool w/adjoining bar and separate wading area for children; tennis courts; small gym w/sauna; travel agency; car rental; salon. *In room:* A/C, TV, coffeemaker, hair dryer, iron, safe.

Rey del Caribe Hotel ★★ *Value* This hotel, located in the center of downtown, is a unique oasis—a 100% ecological hotel, where every detail has been thought out to achieve the goal of living in an organic and environmentally friendly manner. The whole atmosphere of the place is one of warmth, which derives from the on-site owners, who, caring as much as they do for Mother Earth, extend this sentiment to guests as well. You easily forget you're in the midst of downtown Cancún in the tropical jungle setting, with blooming orchids and other flowering plants. Surrounding gardens are populated with statues of Maya deities—it's a lovely, tranquil setting. There's a daily-changing schedule of yoga, Tai Chi, and meditation sessions, as well as special classes on astrology, tarot, and other subjects. Rooms are large and sunny, with your choice of one king or two full-size beds, a kitchenette, and terrace. The detail of ecological sensitivity is truly impressive, ranging from the use of collected rain water to waste composting. Recycling is encouraged and solar power used wherever possible.

Av. Uxmal, corner with Nadar, SM 2-A. ✆ **998/884-2028.** Fax 988/884-9857. www.reycaribe.com. 24 units. High season $63–$100 double; low season $40–$80 double. Rates include breakfast. MC, V. Free parking. **Amenities:** Restaurant; outdoor pool; hot tub; classes. *In room:* A/C, kitchenette.

INEXPENSIVE

Cancún INN Suites El Patio ★ *Finds* Many guests at this small hotel stay for up to a month, drawn by its combination of excellent value and warm hospitality. The European-style guesthouse caters to travelers looking for more of the area's culture. You won't find bars, pools, or loud parties; you will find excellent service and impeccable accommodations. Rooms face the plant-filled interior courtyard, dotted with groupings of wrought-iron chairs and tables. Each room has slightly different appointments and amenities, but all have white tile floors and rustic wood furnishings. Some rooms have kitchenettes, and there's a common kitchen area with purified water and a cooler for stocking your own supplies. There is a public phone in the entranceway, and the staff can arrange for a cellular phone in your room on request. A game and TV room has a large-screen cable TV, a library stocked with books on Mexican culture, backgammon, cards, and board games. While smoking is not allowed in the rooms, it is allowed on the premises.

Av. Bonampak 51 and Cereza, SM2A, Centro, 77500 Cancún, Q. Roo. ✆ **998/884-3500.** Fax 998/884-3540. www.cancun-suites.com. 12 units. $40–$56 double. Spanish-lesson packages available. Ask about discounts for longer stays. AE, MC, V. **Amenities:** Small restaurant (breakfast and dinner). *In room:* A/C, kitchenette, safe.

Hotel Antillano A quiet and very clean choice, the Antillano is close to the Ciudad Cancún bus terminal. Rooms overlook Avenida Tulum, the side streets, or the interior lawn and pool. Pool-view rooms are most desirable because they are quietest. Rooms feature coordinated furnishings, one or two double beds, a sink area separate from the bathroom, and red-tile floors. Guests have the use of the hotel's beach club on the island.

Av. Claveles 1 (corner of Av. Tulum, opposite Restaurant Rosa Mexicana), 77500 Cancún, Q. Roo. ✆ **998/884-1532.** Fax 998/884-1878. www.hotelantillano.com. 48 units. High season $75 double; low season $60 double. AE, MC, V. Street parking. **Amenities:** Small bar; travel agency; babysitting. *In room:* A/C, TV.

Hotel Hacienda Cancún *Value* This extremely pleasing little hotel is a great value. The facade has been remodeled to look like a hacienda. The guest rooms are very comfortable; all have rustic Mexican furnishings and two double beds, but no views. There's a nice small pool and cafe under a shaded *palapa* (an open-sided structure thatched with palm leaves) in the back.

Sunyaxchen 39–40, 77500 Cancún, Q. Roo. ✆ **998/884-3672.** Fax 998/884-1208. hhda@cancun.com.mx. 35 units. High season $45 double; low season $38 double. MC, V. Street parking. From Av. Yaxchilán, turn west on Sunyaxchen; it's on the right next to the Hotel Caribe International, opposite 100% Natural. **Amenities:** Restaurant; pool. *In room:* A/C, TV, safe.

Hotel Margaritas ★ *Value* Located in downtown Cancún, this four-story hotel (with elevator) is comfortable and unpretentious, offering one of the best values in Cancún. The pleasantly decorated rooms, with white tile floors and small balconies, are exceptionally clean and bright. Lounge chairs surround the attractive pool, which has a wading section for children. The hotel offers complimentary safes at the front desk.

Av. Yaxchilán 41, SM22, Centro, 77500 Cancún, Q. Roo. ✆ **01-800/711-1531** in Mexico, or 998/884-9333. Fax 998/884-1324. www.margaritascancun.com. 100 units. High season $85 double; low season $78 double. AE, MC, V. **Amenities:** Restaurant; pool; travel agency; room service; babysitting; medical service; money exchange. *In room:* A/C, TV.

Refugio del Pirata Morgan Although not actually in the town of Cancún, but on the highway leading north from Cancún to Punta Sam, this is the place for those who want a true encounter with nature. Located on a wide, virgin stretch of beach, away from the crowd of hotels and nightlife, this "refuge" is exactly that: no phones, no television, just blissful peace and quiet. There are 10 simple cabañas, with both beds and hammocks, each named for the predominate color of the decor. A small restaurant offers a basic selection of dining choices featuring fresh fish—otherwise, the nearest restaurant is 2km (1¼ miles) away.

Carretera Punta Sam, Isla Blanca, Km 9 77500 Cancún, Q. Roo. ✆ **998/860-3386** (within Mexico dial 044 first, as this is a cellphone). 10 units. $40 room; $5 hammock. **Amenities:** Restaurant. *In room:* Fan.

3 Where to Dine

U.S.-based franchise chains, which really need no introduction, dominate the Cancún restaurant scene. These include Hard Rock Cafe, Rainforest Cafe, Tony Roma's, TGI Friday's, Ruth's Chris Steak House, and the gamut of fast-food burger places. The establishments listed here are locally owned, one-of-a-kind restaurants or exceptional selections at area hotels. Many schedule live music. Unless otherwise indicated, parking is free.

One unique way to combine dinner with sightseeing is aboard the **Lobster Dinner Cruise** (✆ **998/849-4748**). Cruising around the tranquil, turquoise waters of the lagoon, passengers feast on lobster dinners accompanied by wine. Cost is $49 per person. There are two daily departures from the Royal Mayan Marina. A sunset cruise leaves at 4:30pm during the winter and 5:30pm during the summer; a moonlight cruise leaves at 7:30pm winter, 8:30pm summer. Another—albeit livelier—option is the **Captain Hook Lobster Dinner Cruise** (✆ **998/849-4451**), which is similar, but with the added attraction of a pirate show, making this the choice for families. It costs $58 and departs at 7pm from El Embarcadero.

The restaurants of the new Aqua Fiesta Americana (not yet opened at press time) promise to be exceptional, including "7," under the direction of renowned Mexican Chef Patricia Quintana.

CANCUN ISLAND

VERY EXPENSIVE

Aioli ★★★ FRENCH For the quality and originality of the cuisine, coupled with excellent service, this is my top pick for the best fine-dining value in Cancún. The Provençal—but definitely not provincial—Aioli offers exquisite French and Mediterranean gourmet specialties in a warm and cozy country French setting. Though it serves perhaps the best breakfast buffet in Cancún (for $20), most diners from outside the hotel come here in the evening, when low lighting and superb service make it a top choice for a romantic dinner. Starters include traditional pâtés and a delightful escargot served in the shell with white wine and herbed butter sauce. A specialty is duck breast in honey and lavender sauce. Equally scrumptious is rack of lamb, prepared in Moroccan style and served with couscous. Pan-seared grouper is topped with a paste of black olives, crushed potato, and tomato, and bouillabaisse contains an exceptional array of seafood. Desserts are decadent; the signature "Fifth Element" is a sinfully delicious temptation rich with chocolate.

In Le Méridien Cancún Resort & Spa, Retorno del Rey Km 14. ✆ **998/881-2200.** Reservations required. Main courses $14–$30. AE, DC, MC, V. Daily 6:30am–11pm.

Club Grill ★★★ INTERNATIONAL This is the place for that special night out. Cancún's most elegant and stylish restaurant is also among its most delicious. Even rival restaurateurs give it an envious thumbs up. The gracious service starts as you enter the anteroom, with its comfortable seating and selection of fine tequilas and Cuban cigars. It continues in a candlelit dining room with shimmering silver and crystal. Elegant plates of peppered scallops, truffles, and potatoes in tequila sauce; grilled lamb; or mixed grill arrive at a leisurely pace. The restaurant has smoking and nonsmoking sections. A band plays romantic music for dancing from 8pm on.

In the Ritz-Carlton Hotel, Paseo Kukulkán Km 13.5. ✆ **998/881-0808.** Reservations required. No sandals or tennis shoes; men must wear long pants. Main courses $11–$40. AE, DC, MC, V. Tues–Sun 7–11pm.

The Plantation House ★ *Overrated* CARIBBEAN/FRENCH This casually elegant, pale-yellow-and-blue clapboard restaurant overlooking Nichupté lagoon takes you back to the time when the Caribbean first experienced European tastes and culinary talents. The decor combines island-style colonial charm with elegant touches. The service is excellent, but the food is only mediocre, especially considering the price. For starters, try the signature poached shrimp with lemon juice and olive oil, or creamy crabmeat soup. Move on to the main event, which may consist of classic veal Wellington in puff pastry with duck pâté, fish filet crusted in spices and herbs and topped with vanilla sauce, or lobster medallions in mango sauce. Flambéed desserts are a specialty, and the Plantation House has one of the most extensive wine lists in town. It's generally quite crowded, which makes it a bit loud for a romantic evening.

Paseo Kukulkán Km 10.5. ✆ **998/883-1433.** Reservations recommended. Main courses $13–$35. AE, MC, V. Daily 5pm–midnight.

EXPENSIVE

Captain's Cove ★ INTERNATIONAL/SEAFOOD Though it sits almost at the end of Paseo Kukulkán, far from everything, the Captain's Cove continues to pack in customers with its consistent value. Diners sit on several levels, facing big open windows overlooking the lagoon and Royal Yacht Club Marina. For breakfast there's an all-you-can-eat buffet. Main courses of Angus beef and seafood are the norm at lunch and dinner, and there's a children's menu. For dessert there are flaming coffees, crepes, and Key lime pie. The restaurant is on the lagoon side, opposite the Omni Hotel.

Paseo Kukulkán Km 15. ✆ **998/885-0016.** Main courses $12–40; breakfast buffet $10. AE, MC, V. Daily 7am–11pm.

La Dolce Vita ★★★ ITALIAN/SEAFOOD Casually elegant La Dolce Vita is Cancún's favorite Italian restaurant. Appetizers include pâté of quail liver and carpaccio in vinaigrette, and mushrooms Provençal. The chef specializes in homemade pastas combined with fresh seafood. You can order green tagliolini with lobster medallions, linguine with clams or seafood, or rigatoni Mexican-style (with chorizo sausage, mushrooms, and jalapeños) as a main course, or as an appetizer for half price. Other main courses include veal with morels, fresh salmon with cream sauce, and fresh fish in a variety of sauces. Recently added choices include vegetarian lasagna and grilled whole lobster. You have a choice of dining in air-conditioned comfort or on an open-air terrace with a view of the lagoon. Live jazz plays from 7 to 11:30pm Monday through Saturday.

Paseo Kukulkán Km 14.6, on the lagoon, opposite the Marriott Casa Magna. ✆ **998/885-0150** or 998/885-0161. Fax 998/885-0590. www.cancun.com/dining/dolce. Reservations required for dinner. Main courses $9–$29. AE, MC, V. Daily noon–midnight.

Laguna Grill ★★ FUSION Laguna Grill offers diners a contemporary culinary experience in a lush, tropical setting overlooking the lagoon. A tropical garden welcomes you at the entrance, while a small creek traverses through the restaurant set with tables made from the trunks of regional, tropical trees. As magical as the decor is, the real star here is the kitchen, with its offering of Pacific-rim cuisine fused with regional flavors. Starters include martini *gyoza* (steamed dumplings) and shrimp tempura served on a mango mint salad, or ahi tuna and shrimp ceviche in a spicy Oriental sauce. Fish and seafood dominate the menu of entrees, in a variety of preparations that combine Asian and Mexican flavors such as ginger, cilantro, garlic, and hoisin sauce. Grilled shrimp are served over a cilantro and *guajillo* chile risotto. For beef-lovers, the rib-eye served over a garlic, spinach, and sweet potato mash is sublime. Deserts are as creative as the main dishes; the pineapple-papaya strudel in Malibu rum sauce is a standout. If you're an early diner, request a table on the outside deck for a spectacular sunset view. An impressive selection of wines is available.

Bulevar Kukulcán Km 16.5. ✆ **998/885-0267.** www.lagunagrill.com.mx. Reservations recommended. Main courses $15–$45. AE, MC, V. Daily 2pm–midnight.

Lorenzillo's ★★★ *Kids* SEAFOOD This festive, friendly restaurant is a personal favorite—I never miss a lobster stop here when I'm in Cancún. Live lobster is the overwhelming favorite, and part of the appeal is selecting your dinner out of the giant lobster tank. Lorenzillo's sits on the lagoon under a giant *palapa* roof. A dock leads down to the main dining area, and when that's packed (which is often), a wharf-side bar handles the overflow. In addition to lobster—which comes grilled, steamed, or stuffed—good bets are shrimp stuffed with cheese and wrapped in bacon, the Admiral's filet coated in toasted almonds and light mustard sauce, and seafood-stuffed squid. Desserts include the tempting "Martinique": Belgian chocolate with hazelnuts, almonds, and pecans, served with vanilla ice cream. The sunset pier offers a lighter menu of cold seafood, sandwiches, and salads. Children are very welcome.

Paseo Kukulkán Km 10.5. ✆ **998/883-1254.** www.lorenzillos.com.mx. Reservations recommended. Main courses $12–$50. AE, MC, V. Daily noon–midnight. Valet parking available.

Mango Tango ★★ INTERNATIONAL The beauty of dining here is that you can stay and enjoy a hot nightspot—Mango Tango has made a name for itself with sizzling floor shows (featuring salsa, tango, and other Latin dancing) and live reggae music—but its kitchen deserves attention as well. Try the peel-your-own shrimp, Argentine-style grilled meat with *chimichurri* sauce (made with garlic and parsley), and other grilled specialties. Mango Tango salad is shrimp, chicken, avocado, red onion, tomato, and mushrooms served on mango slices. Entrees include rice with seafood and fried bananas. Creole gumbo comes with lobster, shrimp, and squid, and coconut-and-mango cake is a suitable finish to the meal.

Paseo Kukulkán Km 14.2, opposite the Ritz-Carlton Hotel. ✆ **998/885-0303.** Reservations recommended. Main courses $12–$57; 3-course dinner show $40. AE, MC, V. Daily 2pm–2am.

María Bonita ★ Kids REGIONAL/MEXICAN/NOUVELLE MEXICAN In a stylish setting overlooking the water, María Bonita captures the essence of the country through its music and food. Prices are higher and the flavors more institutionalized than at traditional Mexican restaurants in Ciudad Cancún, but this is a good choice for the Hotel Zone. There are three sections: La Cantina Jalisco, with an open kitchen and tequila bar; the Salón Michoacán, which features that state's cuisine; and the Patio Oaxaca. The menu encompasses the best of Mexico's other cuisines, with a few international dishes. Prix-fixe dinners include appetizer, main course, and dessert. Jazz trios, *marimba* and *jarocho* music, and mariachis serenade you while you dine. A nice starter is Mitla salad, with slices of the renowned Oaxaca cheese dribbled with olive oil and coriander dressing. Wonderful stuffed chile La Doña—a mildly hot poblano pepper filled with lobster and *huitlacoche* (a type of mushroom that grows on corn) in a cream sauce—comes as an appetizer or a main course.

In the Hotel Dreams, Punta Cancún (enter from the street). ✆ **998/848-7000,** ext. 8060 or 8061. Reservations recommended. Prix-fixe dinner $30–$45; main courses $17–$31. AE, DC, MC, V. Daily 6:30–11:45pm.

MODERATE

La Destilería MEXICAN If you want to experience tequila in its native habitat, you won't want to miss this place—even though it's across the country from the region that produces the beverage. La Destilería is more than a tequila-inspired restaurant; it's a minimuseum honoring the "spirit" of Mexico. It serves over 150 brands of tequila, including some treasures that never find their way across the country's northern border, so be adventurous! The margaritas are among the best on the island. When you decide to have some food with your tequila, the menu is refined Mexican, with everything from quesadillas with squash blossom flowers, to shrimp in a delicate tequila-lime sauce. They even serve *escamoles* (crisp-fried ant eggs) as an appetizer for the adventurous—or for those whose squeamishness has been diminished by the tequila!

Paseo Kukulkán Km 12.65, across from Plaza Kukulcan. ✆ **998/885-1086** or 998/885-1087. Main courses $8–30. AE, MC, V. Daily 1pm–midnight.

La Fisheria ★ Kids SEAFOOD If you're at the mall shopping, this is your best bet. Patrons find a lot to choose from at this restaurant overlooking Paseo Kukulkán and the lagoon. The expansive menu includes shark fingers with jalapeño dip, grouper filet stuffed with seafood in lobster sauce, Acapulco-style *ceviche* in tomato sauce, New England clam chowder, steamed mussels, grilled red snapper with pasta—you get the idea. The menu changes daily, but there's always *tikin xic,* that great Yucatecan grilled fish marinated in *achiote* (a spice) sauce. For those not inclined toward seafood, a pizza from the wood-burning oven, or perhaps a grilled chicken or beef dish, might do. La Fisheria has a nonsmoking section.

Plaza Caracol shopping center, Paseo Kukulkán Km 8.5, 2nd floor. ✆ **998/883-1395**. Main courses $7–$21. AE, MC, V. Daily 11am–11pm.

Savio's ★ ITALIAN Centrally located at the heart of the Hotel Zone, Savio's is a great place to stop for a quick meal or coffee. Its bar is always crowded with patrons sipping everything from cappuccino to imported beer. Repeat diners look forward to large fresh salads and rich, subtly herb-flavored Italian dishes. Ravioli stuffed with ricotta and spinach comes in delicious tomato sauce. Stylish, with black-and-white decor and tile floors, it has two levels and faces Paseo Kukulkán through two stories of awning-shaded windows.

Plaza Caracol shopping center, Paseo Kukulkán Km 8.5. ✆/fax **998/883-2085.** Main courses $9–$30. AE, MC, V. Daily 10am–midnight.

INEXPENSIVE

100% Natural ★★ VEGETARIAN/MEXICAN If you want a healthy reprieve from an overindulgent night—or just like your meals as fresh and natural as possible—this is your oasis. No matter what your dining preference, you owe it to yourself to try a Mexican tradition, the fresh-fruit *licuado.* The blended drink combines fresh fruit, ice, and either water or milk. More creative combinations may mix in yogurt, granola, or other goodies. And 100% Natural serves more than just meal-quality drinks—there's a bountiful selection of basic Mexican fare and terrific sandwiches served on whole-grain bread, both with options for vegetarians. Breakfast is a delight as well as a good value. The space abounds with plants and cheery colors. There are several locations in town; another is located in Paseo Kukulkán Km 13 (✆ **998/885-2904**) and is open 8am to 11pm.

Plaza Comercial Suite Terramar, next to Plaza Caracol, Local 40–41. ✆ **998/883-3636.** Main courses $2.80–$13. MC, V. Daily 24 hr.

CANCUN CITY

EXPENSIVE

La Habichuela ★ GOURMET SEAFOOD/CARIBBEAN/MEXICAN In a garden setting with soft music playing in the background, this restaurant is ideal for a romantic evening. For an all-out culinary adventure, try *habichuela* (string bean) soup; shrimp in any number of sauces, including Jamaican tamarind, tequila, or ginger-and-mushroom; and Maya coffee with *xtabentun* (a strong, sweet, anise-based liqueur). Grilled seafood and steaks are excellent, but this is a good place to try a Mexican specialty such as *chicken mole* or *tampiqueña*-style beef (thinly sliced, marinated, and grilled). For something totally divine, try *cocobichuela,* which is lobster and shrimp in curry sauce served in a coconut shell and topped with fruit.

Margaritas 25. ✆ **998/884-3158.** habichuela@infosel.net.mx. Reservations recommended in high season. Main courses $10–$32. AE, MC, V. Daily noon–midnight.

Périco's ★★★ MEXICAN/SEAFOOD/STEAKS Périco's has colorful murals that almost dance off the walls, a bar area with saddles for barstools, colorful leather tables and chairs, and accommodating waiters; it's always booming and festive. The extensive menu offers well-prepared steak, seafood, and traditional Mexican dishes for reasonable rates (except for lobster). This is a place not only to eat and drink, but also to let loose and join in the fun, so don't be surprised if everybody drops their forks and dons huge sombreros to shimmy and shake in a conga dance around the dining room. It's fun whether or not you join in, but it's definitely not the place for a romantic evening alone. There's *marimba* music from 7:30 to 9:30pm, and mariachis from 9:30pm to midnight.

Yaxchilán 61. ✆ **998/884-3152.** Reservations recommended. Main courses $9–$39. AE, MC, V. Daily 1pm–1am.

MODERATE

Labná ★ YUCATECAN To steep yourself in Yucatecan cuisine and music, head directly to this showcase of Mayan moods and regional foods. Specialties served here include a sublime lime soup, *poc chuc* (marinated, barbecue-style pork), chicken or pork *pibil* (sweet and spicy barbecue sauce served over shredded meat), and appetizers such as *papadzules* (tortillas stuffed with boiled eggs in a green pumpkin sauce). The Labná Special is a sampler of four typically Yucatecan main courses, including *poc chuc,* while another specialty of the house is baked suckling pig, served with guacamole. The refreshing Yucatecan beverage, *Agua de Chaya*—a blend of sweetened water and the leaf of the Chaya plant, abundant in the area, to which D'aristi liquor can be added for an extra kick—is also served here. The large, informal dining room is decorated with fascinating black and white photographs of the region, dating from the 1900s.

Margaritas 29, next to City Hall and the Habichuela restaurant. ✆ **998/892-3056.** Main courses $5–$18. AE, MC, V. Daily noon–10pm.

Rosa Mexicano ★★ MEXICAN HAUTE CUISINE This beautiful little place has candlelit tables and a plant-filled patio in back, and is almost always packed. Colorful paper banners and piñatas hang from the ceiling, efficient waiters wear bow ties and cummerbunds that match the Mexican flag, and a trio plays romantic Mexican music nightly. The menu features "refined" Mexican specialties. Try *pollo almendro* (chicken covered in cream sauce and sprinkled with ground almonds), or pork baked in a banana leaf with a sauce of oranges, lime, *ancho* chile, and garlic. Steak *tampiqueño* is a huge platter that comes with guacamole salad, quesadillas, beans, salad, and rice.

Claveles 4. ✆ **998/884-6313.** Fax 998/884-2371. Reservations recommended for parties of 6 or more. Main courses $9–$17; lobster $30. AE, MC, V. Daily 5–11pm.

Stefano's ITALIAN/PIZZA Call the food Mexitalian if you will, but it seems to be a winning combination. Stefano's began primarily as a local restaurant, serving Italian food with a few Mexican accents, and is now equally popular with tourists. Among the menu items are ravioli stuffed with *huitlacoche* (a type of mushroom that grows on corn); rigatoni in tequila sauce; and seafood with chile peppers, nestled proudly alongside the Stefano special pizza, made with fresh tomato, cheese, and pesto. For dessert, ricotta strudel is something out of the ordinary. Stefano's offers lots of different coffees and mixed drinks, plus an expanded wine list.

Bonampak 177. ✆ **998/887-9964.** Main courses $7–$17; pizza $6–$17. AE, MC, V. Daily 1pm–midnight.

INEXPENSIVE

Pizza Rolandi *Kids* ITALIAN This is an institution in Cancún, and the Rolandi name is synonymous with dependable, casual dining in both Cancún and neighboring Isla Mujeres. At this shaded outdoor patio restaurant, you can choose from almost two dozen wood-oven pizzas and a full selection of spaghetti, calzones, Italian-style chicken and beef, and desserts. There's a full bar as well.

Cobá 12. ✆ **998/884-4047.** Fax 998/884-3994. www.rolandi.com. Pasta $5–$8; pizza and main courses $7–$14. AE, MC, V. Daily noon–11pm.

3 What to See & Do in Cancún

You will run out of vacation days before you run out of things to do in Cancún. Snorkeling, jet-skiing, jungle tours, and visits to ancient Maya ruins and modern ecological theme parks are among the most popular diversions. There are a dozen malls with name-brand and duty-free shops (with European goods at prices better than in the U.S.), and more than 350 restaurants and nightclubs. The 24,000-plus hotel rooms in the area offer something for every taste and every budget.

In addition to having attractions of its own, Cancún is a convenient distance from the more traditional resorts of Isla Mujeres and from the coastal zone now known as the Riviera Maya—extending down from Cancún, through Playa del Carmen, to the Maya ruins at Tulum, Cozumel, Chichén Itzá, and Cobá. All are within day-trip distance. Isla Mujeres and destinations along the Riviera Maya are discussed in chapter 4. Tulum, Chichén Itzá, and Cobá are discussed in chapter 5. For more on Cozumel, please see *Frommer's Cancún, Cozumel & the Yucatán.*

1 Beaches, Watersports & Boat Tours

THE BEACHES

Big hotels dominate the best stretches of beach. All of Mexico's beaches are public property, so you can use the beach of any hotel by walking through the lobby or directly onto the sand. Be especially careful on beaches fronting the open Caribbean, where the undertow can be quite strong. By contrast, the waters of Mujeres Bay (Bahía de Mujeres), at the north end of the island, are usually calm and ideal for swimming. Get to know Cancún's water-safety pennant system, and make sure to check the flag at any beach or hotel before entering the water. Here's how it goes:

- **White** Excellent
- **Green** Normal conditions (safe)
- **Yellow** Changeable, uncertain (use caution)
- **Black** or **red** Unsafe; use the swimming pool instead!

In the Caribbean, storms can arrive and conditions can change from safe to unsafe in a matter of minutes, so be alert: If you see dark clouds heading your way, make for the shore and wait until the storm passes.

Playa Tortuga (Turtle Beach), Playa Langosta (Lobster Beach), Playa Linda (Pretty Beach), and **Playa Las Perlas (Beach of the Pearls)** are some of the public beaches. At most beaches, you can rent a sailboard and take lessons, ride a parasail, or partake in a variety of watersports. There's a small but beautiful portion of public beach on **Playa Caracol,** by the Xcaret Terminal. It faces the calm waters of Bahía de Mujeres and, for that reason, is preferable to those facing the Caribbean.

WATERSPORTS

Many beachside hotels offer watersports concessions that rent rubber rafts, kayaks, and snorkeling equipment. On the calm Nichupté lagoon are outlets for renting **sailboats, jet skis, windsurfers,** and **water skis.** Prices vary and are often negotiable, so check around.

DEEP-SEA FISHING

You can arrange a day of **deep-sea fishing** at one of the numerous piers or travel agencies for around $220 to $360 for 4 hours, $420 for 6 hours, and $520 for 8 hours for up to four people. Marinas will sometimes assist in putting together a group. Charters include a captain, a first mate, bait, gear, and beverages. Rates are lower if you depart from Isla Mujeres or from Cozumel—and frankly, the fishing is better closer to those departure points.

SCUBA & SNORKELING

Known for its shallow reefs, dazzling color, and diversity of life, Cancún is one of the best places in the world for beginning **scuba diving.** Punta Nizuc is the northern tip of the **Gran Arrecife Maya (Great Mesoamerican Reef),** the largest reef in the Western Hemisphere and one of the largest in the world. In addition to the sea life along this reef system, several sunken boats add a variety of dive options. Inland, a series of caverns and *cenotes* (sinkholes or wellsprings with deep blue waters) are fascinating venues for the more experienced diver. Drift diving is the norm here, with popular dives going to the reefs at **El Garrafón** and the **Caves of the Sleeping Sharks**—although be aware that the famed "sleeping sharks" have departed, driven off by too many people watching them snooze.

A variety of hotels offer resort courses that teach the basics of diving—enough to make shallow dives and slowly ease your way into this underwater world of unimaginable beauty. Scuba trips run around $64 for two-tank dives at nearby reefs, and $100 and up for locations farther out. **Scuba Cancún,** Paseo Kukulkán Km 5 (✆ **998/849-7508** or 998/849-4736 for reservations; www.scubacancun.com.mx), on the lagoon side, offers a 4-hour resort course for $84. Phone reservations are available from 7:30 to 10:30pm. Full certification takes 4 to 5 days and costs around $368. Scuba Cancún is open daily from 9am to 6pm, and accepts major credit cards. The largest operator is **Aquaworld,** across from the Meliá Cancún at Paseo Kukulkán Km 15.2 (✆ **998/848-8300** or 998/848-8327; www.aquaworld.com.mx). It offers resort courses and diving from a man-made anchored dive platform, Paradise Island. Aquaworld has the **Sub See Explorer,** a boat with picture windows that hang beneath the surface. The boat doesn't submerge—it's an updated version of a glass-bottom boat—but it does provide nondivers with a look at life beneath the sea. This outfit is open 24 hours a day and accepts all major credit cards.

Scuba Cancún also offers diving trips, in good weather only, to 20 nearby reefs, including Cuevones (9m/30 ft.) and the open ocean (9–18m/30–60 ft.). The average dive is around 11m (35 ft.). One-tank dives cost $55, and two-tank dives cost $65. Discounts apply if you bring your own equipment. Dives usually start around 10am and return by 2:15pm. Snorkeling trips cost $27 and leave every afternoon after 1:30pm for shallow reefs about a 20-minute boat ride away.

Besides **snorkeling** at **El Garrafón Natural Park** (see "Boating Tours," below), travel agencies offer an all-day excursion to the natural wildlife habitat of **Isla Contoy,** which usually includes time for snorkeling. The island, 90 minutes past Isla Mujeres, is a major nesting area for birds and a treat for nature lovers. You can call any travel agent or see any hotel tour desk to get a selection of boat tours to **Isla Contoy.** Prices range from $44 to $65, depending on the length of the trip, and generally include drinks and snorkeling equipment.

The Great Mesoamerican Reef also offers exceptional snorkeling opportunities. In Puerto Morelos, 37km (23 miles) south of Cancún, the reef hugs the coastline for 15km (9 miles). The reef is so close to the shore (about 460m/1,500 ft.) that it forms a natural barrier for the village and keeps the waters calm on the inside of the reef. The water here is shallow, from 1.5 to 9m (5–30 ft.), resulting in ideal conditions for snorkeling. Stringent environmental regulations implemented by the local community have kept the reef here unspoiled. Only a select few companies are allowed to offer snorkel trips, and they must adhere to guidelines that will ensure the reef's preservation. **Cancún Mermaid** (✆ **998/843-6517;** www.cancun mermaid.com) is considered the best—it's a family-run ecotour company that has operated in the area since the 1970s. It's known for highly personalized service. The tour typically takes snorkelers to two sections of the reef, spending about an hour in each area. When conditions allow, the boat drops off snorkelers and then follows them along with the current—an activity known as "drift snorkeling," which enables snorkelers to see as much of the reef as possible. The trip costs $50 for adults, $35 for children, which includes boat, snorkeling gear, life jackets, a light lunch, bottled water, sodas, and beer, plus round-trip transportation to and from Puerto Morelos from Cancún hotels. Departures are Monday through Saturday at 9am or noon, a minimum of four snorkelers is required for a trip, and reservations are required.

JET SKI TOURS

Several companies offer the popular **Jungle Cruise,** which takes you by jet ski or WaveRunner (you drive your own watercraft) through Cancún's lagoon and mangrove estuaries out into the Caribbean Sea and a shallow reef. The excursion runs about 2½ hours and costs $35 to $45, including snorkeling and beverages. Some of the motorized miniboats seat one person behind the other—meaning that the person in back gets a great view of the driver's head; others seat you side by side.

The operators and names of boats offering excursions change often. To find out what's available, check with a local travel agent or hotel tour desk. The popular **Aquaworld,** Paseo Kukulkán Km 15.2 (✆ **998/848-8300,** or 998/885-2288), calls its trip the Jungle Tour and charges $45 for the 2½-hour excursion, which includes 45 minutes of snorkeling time. It even gives you a free snorkel, but has the less-desirable one-behind-the-other seating configuration. Departures are 8am, 8:30, 9, 10:30, and 11:30am, noon, 1, 2, 2:30, 3:30, and 4:30pm daily.

BOATING TOURS

TO ISLA MUJERES

The island of **Isla Mujeres,** just 13km (8 miles) offshore, is one of the most pleasant day trips from Cancún. At one end is **El Garrafón Natural Park,** which is excellent for snorkeling. At the other end is a captivating village with small shops, restaurants, and hotels, and **Playa Norte,** the island's best beach. If you're looking for relaxation and can spare the time, it's worth several days. For more information about the island, see chapter 4.

There are four ways to get there: **public ferry** from Puerto Juárez, which takes between 15 and 45 minutes; **shuttle boat** from Playa Linda or Playa Tortuga—an hour-long ride, with irregular service; **Water Taxi** (more expensive, but faster), next to the Xcaret Terminal; and daylong **pleasure-boat trips,** most of which leave from the Playa Linda pier.

The inexpensive Puerto Juárez **public ferries** ★ are just a few kilometers from downtown Cancún. From Cancún City, take the Ruta 8 bus on Avenida Tulum to Puerto Juárez. The air-conditioned *Caribbean Express* (20 min.) costs $4 per person. Departures are every half-hour from 6 to 8:30am and then every 15 minutes until 8:30pm. The slower *Caribbean Savage* (45–60 min.) is a bargain at about $2. It departs every 2 hours, or less frequently depending on demand. Upon arrival, the ferry docks in downtown Isla Mujeres near all the shops, restaurants, hotels, and Norte beach. You'll need a taxi to get to El Garrafón park, at the other end of the island. You can stay as long as you like on the island (even overnight) and return by ferry, but be sure to double-check the time of the last returning ferry.

Pleasure-boat cruises to Isla Mujeres are a favorite pastime. Modern motor yachts, catamarans, trimarans, and even old-time sloops—more than 25 boats a day—take swimmers, sun lovers, snorkelers, and shoppers out on the translucent waters. Some tours include a snorkeling stop at El Garrafón, lunch on the beach, and a short time for shopping in downtown Isla Mujeres. Most leave at 9:30 or 10am, last about 5 or 6 hours, and include continental breakfast, lunch, and rental of snorkel gear. Others, particularly sunset and night cruises, go to beaches away from town for pseudo-pirate shows and include a lobster dinner or Mexican buffet. If you want to actually see Isla Mujeres, go on a morning cruise, or travel on your own using the public ferry from Puerto Juárez. Prices for the day cruises run around $45 per person.

TO EL GARRAFON

El Garrafón Natural Park ★★ is under the same management as Xcaret (✆ **998/884-9422;** see chapter 4). The basic entrance fee of $29 includes access to the reef and a museum, as well as use of kayaks, inner tubes, life vests, the pool, hammocks, and public facilities and showers. Snorkel gear and lockers can be rented for an extra charge. There are also nature trails as well as several restaurants on-site. An all-inclusive option is available for $59, which includes dining on

Tips An All-Terrain Tour

Cancún Mermaid (✆ **998/843-6517** or 998/886-4117; www.cancunmermaid.com), in Cancún, offers all-terrain-vehicle (ATV) jungle tours for $49 per person. The ATV tours travel through the jungles of Cancún and emerge on the beaches of the Riviera Maya. The 2½-hour tour includes equipment, instruction, the services of a tour guide, and bottled water; it departs daily at 8am and 1:30pm. The company picks you up at your hotel. Another ATV option is Rancho Loma Bonita; see "Horseback Riding," below.

whatever you choose at any of the restaurants, plus unlimited domestic drinks and use of snorkel gear, locker, and towel. El Garrafón also has full dive facilities and gear rentals, plus an expansive gift shop.

TO THE REEFS

Other excursions go to the **reefs** in glass-bottom boats, so you can have a near-scuba-diving experience and see many colorful fish. However, the reefs are some distance from the shore and are impossible to reach on windy days with choppy seas. They've also suffered from overvisitation, and their condition is far from pristine. Nautibus's **Atlantis Submarine** (✆ **987/872-5671**) takes you close to the aquatic action. Departures vary, depending on weather conditions. Prices are $81 for adults, $48 for children ages 4 to 12. The submarine descends to a depth of 30m (100 ft.). Atlantis Submarine departs Monday to Saturday every hour from 8am until 2pm; the tour lasts about an hour. The submarine departs from Cozumel, so you either need to take a ferry to get there or purchase the package that includes round-trip ground and water transportation from your hotel in Cancún ($103 adults, $76 children 4–12). Reservations are recommended.

2 Outdoor Activities & Attractions

OUTDOOR ACTIVITIES

DOLPHIN SWIMS

On Isla Mujeres, you have the opportunity to swim with dolphins at **Dolphin Discovery** ★ (✆ **998/849-4757;** fax 998/849-4758; www.dolphindiscovery.com). There are several options for dolphin interaction, but my choice is the Royal Swim, which includes an educational introduction followed by 30 minutes of swim time. The price is $125 (MasterCard and Visa are accepted), with transportation to Isla Mujeres an additional $5 for program participants. Advance reservations are required. Assigned swimming times are 10am, noon, 2, or 3:30pm, and you must arrive 1½ hour before your scheduled swim time. In Cancún, the **Parque Nizuc** (✆ **998/881-3030**) marine park offers guests a chance to swim with dolphins and view them in their dolphin aquarium, Atlántida. The price of the dolphin swim ($135) includes admission to the park. It's a fun place for a family to spend the day, with its numerous pools, waterslides, and rides. Visitors can also snorkel with manta rays, tropical fish, and tame sharks. It's at the southern end of Cancún, between the airport and the Hotel Zone. Admission is $27 for adults, $23 for children 3 to 11 (American Express, MasterCard, and Visa are accepted). Open daily from 10am to 5:30pm.

La Isla Shopping Center, Bulevar Kukulkán Km 12.5, has an impressive **Interactive Aquarium** (✆ **998/883-0411,** 998/883-0436, or 998/883-0413; www.aquariumcancun.com.mx) with dolphin swims and the chance to feed a shark while immersed in the water in an acrylic cage. Guides inside the main tank use underwater microphones to point out the sea life, and even answer your questions. Open exhibition tanks enable visitors to touch a variety of marine life, including sea stars and manta rays. The educational dolphin program is $55, while the dolphin swim is $115. The entrance fee to the aquarium is $6 for adults, $4 for children, and it's open from 9am to 7pm, daily.

GOLF & TENNIS

The 18-hole **Pok-Ta-Pok Club,** or Club de Golf Cancún (✆ **998/883-0871**), a Robert Trent Jones, Sr., design, is on the northern leg of the island. Greens fees run $100 per 18 holes, with clubs renting for $26 and shoes for $15. Hiring a caddy costs $20. The club is open daily, accepts American Express, MasterCard, and Visa, and has tennis courts.

The **Hilton Cancún Golf & Beach Resort** (✆ **998/881-8016;** fax 998/881-8084) has a championship 18-hole, par-72 course designed around the Ruinas Del Rey. Greens fees for the public are $125 for 18 holes and $99 for 9 holes; Hilton Cancún guests receive a 20% discount off these rates, which includes a golf cart. Golf clubs and shoes are available for rent. The club is open daily from 6am to 6pm.

The **Meliá Cancún** (✆ **998/881-1100,** ext. 193) has a 9-hole executive course; the fee is $43. The club is open daily from 7am to 4:30pm and accepts American Express, MasterCard, and Visa.

The first Jack Nicklaus Signature Golf Course in the Cancún area has opened at the **Moon Palace Golf Resort,** along the Riviera Maya (www.palaceresorts.com). Two additional PGA courses are planned for the area just north of Cancún, Puerto Cancún, in 2007 and 2008.

HORSEBACK RIDING

Rancho Loma Bonita (✆ **998/887-5465** or 998/887-5423; www.lomabonitamex.com), about 30 minutes south of town, is Cancún's most popular option for horseback riding. Five-hour packages include 2 hours of riding through the mangrove swamp to the beach, where you have time to swim and relax. The tour costs $72 for adults, $65 for children 6 to 12. The ranch also offers a four-wheel ATV ride on the same route as the horseback tour. It costs $72 per person if you want to ride on your own, $55 if you double up. Prices for both tours include transportation to the ranch, riding, soft drinks, and lunch, plus a guide and insurance. Visa is accepted, but cash is preferred.

ATTRACTIONS IN & AROUND TOWN

A MUSEUM

To the right side of the entrance to the Cancún Convention Center is the **Museo Arqueológico de Cancún** (✆ **998/883-0305**), a small but interesting museum with relics from archaeological sites around the state. Admission is $3; free on Sunday and holidays. It's open Tuesday through Friday from 9am to 8pm, Saturday and Sunday from 10am to 7pm.

Another cultural enclave is the **Museo de Arte Popular Mexicano** (✆ **998/849-4848**), located at on the second floor of the El Embarcadero Marina, km 4, Paseo Kukulkán. It displays a representative collection of masks, regional folkloric costumes, nativity scenes, religious artifacts, musical instruments, Mexican toys, and gourd art, spread over 1,370 sq. m (4,500 sq. ft.) of exhibition space. Admission is $10, with kids under 12 paying half price. The museum is open daily from 11am to 11pm.

BULLFIGHTS

Cancún has a small bullring, **Plaza de Toros** (✆ **998/884-8372;** bull@prodigy.net.mx), near the northern (town) end of Paseo Kukulkán opposite the Restaurant Los Almendros. Bullfights take place every Wednesday at 3:30pm during the winter tourist season. A sport introduced to Mexico by the Spanish viceroys, bullfighting is now as much a part of Mexican culture as tequila. The bullfights usually include four bulls, and the spectacle begins with a folkloric dance exhibition, followed by a performance by the *charros* (Mexico's sombrero-wearing cowboys). You're not likely to see Mexico's best bullfights in Cancún—the real stars are in Mexico City. Keep in mind that if you go to a bullfight, *you're going to see a bullfight,* so stay away if you're an animal lover or you can't bear the sight of blood. Travel agencies in Cancún sell tickets, which cost $35 for adults, free for children under 6; seating is by general admission. American Express, MasterCard, and Visa are accepted.

SIGHTSEEING

Get the best possible view of Cancún atop the **La Torre Cancún,** Paseo Kukulkán Km 4 (✆ **998/849-4848**), a rotating tower at the El Embarcadero park and entertainment complex. One ride costs $9; a day and night pass goes for $14. Open daily from 9am to 11pm.

3 Shopping

Despite the surrounding natural splendor, shopping has become a favorite activity. Cancún is known throughout Mexico for its diverse shops and festive malls catering to a large number of international tourists. Visitors from the United States may find apparel more expensive in Cancún, but the selection is much broader than at other Mexican resorts. Numerous duty-free shops offer excellent value on European goods. The largest is **UltraFemme,** Avenida Tulum, Supermanzana 25 (✆ **998/884-1402** or 998/885-0804), specializing in imported cosmetics, perfumes, and fine jewelry and watches. The downtown Cancún location offers slightly lower prices than branches in Plaza Caracol, Plaza Kukulcan, Plaza Mayafair, Flamingo Plaza, and the international airport.

Handicrafts are more limited and more expensive in Cancún than in other regions of Mexico because they are not produced here. They are available, though; several **open-air crafts markets** are on Avenida Tulum in Cancún City and near the convention center in the Hotel Zone. One of the biggest is **Coral Negro,** Paseo Kukulkán Km 9.5 (✆ **998/883-0758;** fax 998/883-0758), open daily from 7am to 11pm. A small restaurant inside, Xtabentun, serves Yucatecan food and pizza slices, and metamorphoses into a dance club around 9 or 10pm.

Cancún's main venues are the **malls**—not quite as grand as their U.S. counterparts, but close. All are air-conditioned, sleek, and sophisticated. Most are on Paseo Kukulkán between Km 7 and Km

12. They offer everything from fine crystal and silver to designer clothing and decorative objects, along with numerous restaurants and clubs. Stores are generally open daily from 10am to 10pm.

The **Plaza Kukulcan** (✆ **998/885-2200;** www.kukulcan plaza.com) offers a large selection—more than 300—of shops, restaurants, and entertainment. There's a branch of Banco Serfin; OK Maguey Cantina Grill; a theater with U.S. movies; an Internet access kiosk; Tikal, which sells Guatemalan textile clothing; several crafts stores; a liquor store; several bathing-suit specialty stores; record and tape outlets; a leather goods store (including shoes and sandals); and a store specializing in silver from Taxco. The Fashion Gallery features designer clothing. In the food court are a number of U.S. franchise restaurants, including Ruth's Chris Steak House, plus one featuring specialty coffee. There's also a large indoor parking garage. The mall is open daily from 10am to 10pm, until 11pm during high season. Assistance for those with disabilities is available upon request, and wheelchairs, strollers, and lockers are available at the information desk.

Planet Hollywood anchors the **Plaza Flamingo** (✆ **998/883-2945**), which has branches of Bancrecer, Subway, and La Casa del Habano (Cuban cigars).

The long-standing **Plaza Caracol** (✆ **998/883-1038**) holds Cartier jewelry, Guess, Waterford Crystal, Señor Frog's clothing, Samsonite luggage, and La Fisheria restaurant. It's just before you reach the convention center as you come from downtown Cancún.

Maya Fair Plaza/Centro Comercial Maya Fair, frequently called "Mayfair" (✆ **998/883-2801**), is the oldest mall. The lively center holds open-air restaurants and bars, including the Outback Steakhouse and Sanborn's Café, and several stores sell silver, leather, and crafts.

The entertainment-oriented **Forum by the Sea,** Paseo Kukulkán Km 9 (✆ **998/883-4425**), has shops including Tommy Hilfiger, Levi's, Diesel, Swatch, and Harley Davidson. Most people come here for the food and fun, choosing from Hard Rock Cafe, Coco Bongo, Rainforest Cafe, Sushi-ito, and Santa Fe Beer Factory, plus an extensive food court. It's open daily from 10am to midnight (bars remain open later).

The newest and most intriguing mall is the **La Isla Shopping Village,** Paseo Kukulkán Km 12.5 (✆ **998/883-5025;** www.laisla cancun.com.mx), an open-air festival mall that looks like a small village. Walkways lined with shops and restaurants cross little canals.

It also has a "riverwalk" alongside the Nichupté lagoon, and an interactive aquarium and dolphin swim facility, as well as the Spacerocker and River Ride Tour—great for kid-friendly fun. Shops include Guess, Diesel, DKNY, Guess, Bulgari, and Ultra Femme. Dining choices include Johnny Rockets, Come and Eat, Häagen-Dazs, and the beautiful Mexican restaurant La Casa de las Margaritas. You also can find a movie theater, a video arcade, and several nightclubs, including Glazz. It's across from the Sheraton, on the lagoon side of the street.

4 Cancún After Dark

One of Cancún's main draws is its active nightlife. The hottest centers of action are the **Centro Comercial Maya Fair, Forum by the Sea,** and **La Isla Shopping Village.** Hotels also compete, with happy-hour entertainment and special drink prices to entice visitors and guests from other resorts. (Lobby bar–hopping at sunset is one great way to plan next year's vacation.)

THE CLUB & MUSIC SCENE

Clubbing in Cancún is a favorite part of the vacation experience and can go on each night until the sun rises over that incredibly blue sea. Several big hotels have nightclubs or schedule live music in their lobby bars. At the clubs, expect to stand in long lines on weekends, pay a cover charge of $15 to $25 per person, and pay $5 to $8 for a drink. Some of the higher-priced clubs include an open bar or live entertainment. The places listed in this section are air-conditioned and accept American Express, MasterCard, and Visa.

A great idea to get you started is the **Bar Leaping Tour** ★★ (**© 998/883-5402**). For $49, it takes you by way of the *Froguibus* from bar to club—the list currently includes Señor Frog's, Glazz, and Coco Bongo—where you'll bypass any lines and spend about 2 hours in each place. The price includes entry to the clubs, one welcome drink at each, and transportation by air-conditioned bus, allowing you to get a great sampling of the best of Cancún's nightlife. The tour runs from 8pm to 3:30am, with the meeting point at Come and Eat restaurant in the La Isla Hopping Village. American Express, Visa, and MasterCard, are accepted.

Numerous restaurants, such as **Carlos 'n Charlie's, Hard Rock Cafe, Señor Frog's, TGI Friday's,** and **Iguana Wana,** double as nighttime party spots, offering wild-ish fun at a fraction of the price of more costly clubs.

Bulldog Café, Paseo Kukulkán Km 7.5 (© **998/848-9800**), is an impressive space with room for over 2,000 revelers and features signature laser-light shows, infused oxygen, large video screens, and even a VIP Jacuzzi for some truly interesting nocturnal fun. The overall ambience is casual and funky. The music ranges from hip-hop to Latino rock, with a heavy emphasis on infectious dance tunes. Bulldog opens at 10 p.m. nightly and stays open until the party winds down. The cover charge is $12 per person or pay $25 for open bar all night long (domestic drinks only).

The City ★★★, Bulevar Kukulcán Km 9.5 (© **998/848-8380;** www.thecitycancun.com), is currently Cancún's hottest club, featuring progressive electronic music spun by some of the world's top DJs. With visiting DJs from New York, L.A., and Mexico City—Moby even played here—the music is sizzling. You actually need never leave, as The City is a day-and-night club. The City Beach Club opens at 8am, and features a pool with a wave machine for surfing and boogie-boarding, a tower-high waterslide, food and bar service, plus beach cabañas. The Terrace Bar, overlooking the action on Bulevar Kukulcán, serves food and drinks all day long. For a relaxing evening vibe, the Lounge features comfy couches, chill music, and an extensive menu of martinis, snacks, and deserts. Open at 10pm, the 7,600-sq.-m (25,000-sq.-ft.) nightclub has nine bars, stunning light shows, and several VIP areas. Located in front of Coco Bongo, The City also has a second location in Playa del Carmen.

Carlos 'n Charlie's, Paseo Kukulkán Km 4.5 (© **998/883-1862**), is a reliable place to find both good food and packed-frat-house entertainment in the evening. There's a dance floor; live music starts nightly around 8:30pm. A cover charge kicks in if you're not planning to eat. It's open daily from 11am to 2am.

With recorded music, **Carlos O'Brian's,** Tulum 107, SM 22 (© **998/883-1092**), is only slightly tamer than other Carlos Anderson restaurants and nightspots in town (Señor Frog's and Carlos 'n' Charlie's). It's open daily from 9am to midnight.

Continuing its reputation as one of the hottest spots in town is **Coco Bongo** ★★ in Forum by the Sea, Paseo Kukulkán Km 9.5 (© **998/883-5061;** www.cocobongo.com.mx). Its main appeal is that it has no formal dance floor, so you can dance anywhere—and that includes on the tables, on the bar, or even on the stage with the live band! This place can—and regularly does—pack in up to 3,000 people. You have to experience it to believe it. Despite its capacity, lines are long on weekends and in high season. The music alternates between Caribbean, salsa, house, hip-hop, techno, and classics from the 1970s and '80s. It draws a mixed crowd, but the young and hip dominate. Choose between a $15 cover or $25 with an open bar.

Dady'O, Paseo Kukulkán Km 9.5 (© **998/883-3333**), is a highly favored rave with frequent long lines. It opens nightly at 10pm and generally charges a cover of $15.

Dady Rock Bar and Grill, Paseo Kukulkán Km 9.5 (© **998/883-1626**), the offspring of Dady'O, opens at 6pm and goes as long as any other nightspot, offering a combination of live bands and DJs spinning music, along with an open bar, full meals, a buffet, and dancing.

Glazz, in La Isla Shopping Village, Bulevar Kukulcán Km 12.5, Local B-7 (© **998/883-1881;** www.glazz.com.mx), is Cancún's newest nocturnal offering, combining a restaurant with a sleek lounge and sophisticated nightclub for a complete evening of entertainment. Geared for those over 30, music is mostly lounge and house, and there are live entertainment acts (anything from drummers to sultry dancers) periodically through the evening. The staff is known as being among the top in town. The China Bistro is already earning rave reviews, while the Lounge's vast selection of martinis and tequilitinis is dangerously tempting. The Club is pure Miami-style, with plenty of neon and a very hot DJ. It's open nightly from 7pm to 5am. Cover is $10, and a dress code prohibits sandals or shorts.

Hard Rock Cafe, in Plaza Lagunas Mall and Forum by the Sea (© **998/881-8120** or 998/883-2024; www.hardrock.com), schedules a live band at 10:30pm Thursday through Tuesday night. At other times you get lively recorded music to munch by—the menu combines the most popular foods from American and Mexican cultures. It's open daily from 11am to 2am.

La Boom, Paseo Kukulkán Km 3.5 (© **998/883-1152;** fax 998/883-1458; www.laboom.com.mx), has two sections: One side is a video bar, the other a bi-level dance club with cranking music. Each night there's a special deal: no cover, free bar, ladies' night, bikini night, and others. Popular with early-20-somethings, it's open nightly from 10pm to 6am. A sound-and-light show begins at 11:30pm in the dance club. The cover varies depending on the night—most nights women enter free, and men pay $15 to $30, which includes an open bar.

The most refined and upscale of Cancún's nightly gathering spots is the **Lobby Lounge** at the **Ritz-Carlton Hotel** ★ (✆ **998/885-0808**), with live dance music and a list of more than 120 premium tequilas for tasting or sipping.

THE PERFORMING ARTS

Several hotels host **Mexican fiesta nights,** including a buffet dinner and a folkloric dance show; admission, including dinner, ranges from $35 to $50.

You can also get in the party mood at **Mango Tango** ★, Paseo Kukulkán Km 14.2 (✆ **998/885-0303**), a lagoon-side restaurant and dinner-show establishment opposite the Ritz-Carlton Hotel. Diners can choose from two levels, one nearer the music and the other overlooking it all. Music is loud and varied but mainly features reggae or salsa. A 45-minute floor show starts nightly at 8:30pm. A variety of packages are available—starting at $40 per person—depending on whether you want dinner and the show, open bar and the show, or the show alone. For dancing, which starts at 9:30, there's a $10 cover charge. See "Where to Dine," in chapter 2, for a restaurant review.

Tourists mingle with locals at the downtown **Parque de las Palapas** (the main park) for *Noches Caribeñas,* which involves free live tropical music for anyone who wants to listen and dance. Performances begin at 7:30pm on Sunday, and sometimes there are performances on Friday and Saturday.

4

Day Trips: Island Getaways & Nature Parks

One of the best ways to spend a vacation day is exploring the nearby archaeological ruins or an ecological theme park near Cancún. Within easy driving distance are historical and natural treasures unlike any you've likely encountered before. Cancún can be a perfect base for day or overnight trips, or the starting point for a longer expedition.

This chapter discusses **Isla Mujeres, Xel-Ha,** and **Xcaret.** For those who truly want to get a way from it all, I've also included information about the rustic natural beauty of the **Punta Allen Peninsula.** For information on the Maya ruins to the south at **Tulum** or **Cobá,** see chapter 5.

1 Isla Mujeres ★★★

16km (10 miles) N of Cancún

Isla Mujeres (Island of Women) is a casual, laid-back refuge from the conspicuously commercialized action of Cancún, visible across a narrow channel. It's known as the best value in the Caribbean, assuming that you favor an easy-going vacation pace and prefer simplicity to pretense. This is an island of white-sand beaches and turquoise waters, complemented by a town filled with Caribbean-colored clapboard houses and rustic, open-air restaurants. Hotels are clean and comfortable, but if you're looking for lots of action or opulence, you'll be happier in Cancún. A few recent additions provide more luxurious lodging, but they still maintain a decidedly casual atmosphere.

Francisco Hernández de Córdoba, seeing figurines of partially clad females along the shore, gave the island its name when he landed in 1517. These are now believed to have been offerings to the Maya goddess of fertility and the moon, Ixchel. Their presence indicates that the island was probably sacred to the Maya.

The Yucatán's Upper Caribbean Coast

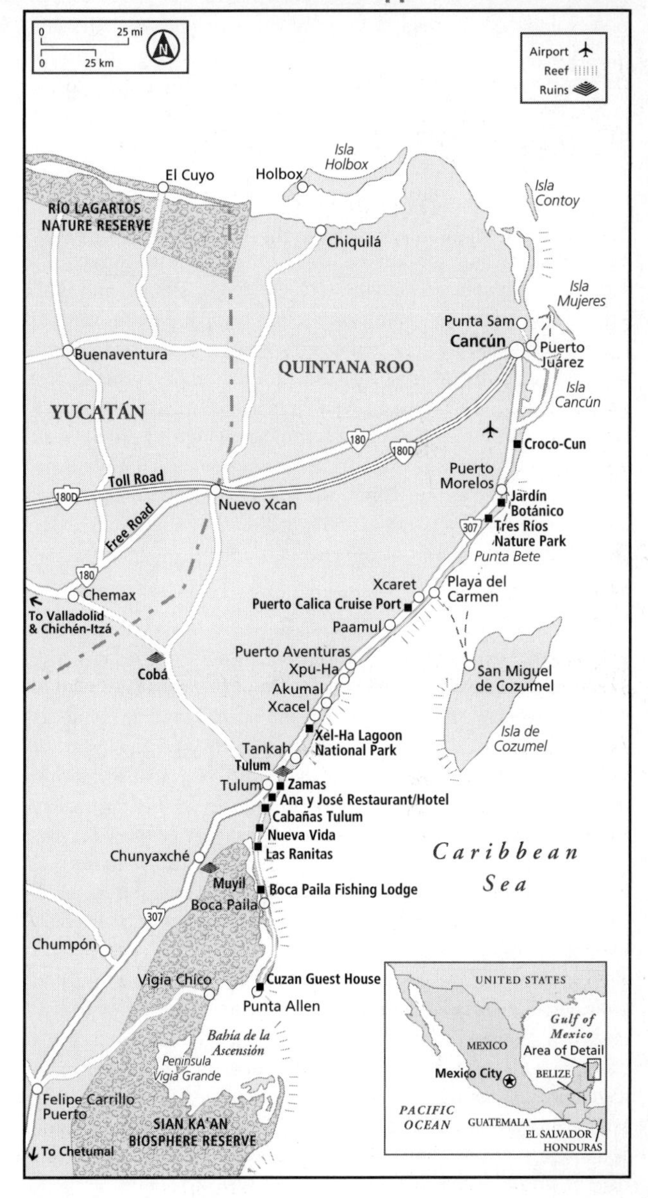

At midday, suntanned visitors hang out in open-air cafes and stroll streets lined with frantic souvenir vendors. Calling attention to their bargain-priced wares, they give a carnival atmosphere to the hours when tour-boat traffic is at its peak. Befitting the size of the island, most of the traffic consists of golf carts, *motos* (mopeds), and bicycles. Once the tour boats leave, however, Isla Mujeres reverts to its more typical, tranquil way of life.

Days in "Isla"—as the locals call it—can alternate between adventurous activity and absolute repose. Trips to the Isla Contoy bird sanctuary are popular, as are the excellent diving, fishing, and snorkeling—in 1998, the island's coral coast became part of Mexico's Marine National Park. The island and several of its traditional hotels attract regular gatherings of yoga practitioners. In the evening, most people find the slow, casual pace one of the island's biggest draws. The cool night breeze is a perfect accompaniment to casual open-air dining and drinking in small street-side restaurants. Many people pack it in as early as 9 or 10pm, when most of the businesses close. Those in search of a party, however, will find kindred souls at the bars on Playa Norte that stay open late.

ESSENTIALS

GETTING THERE & DEPARTING From mainland Cancún, **Isla Mujeres** is an easy and enjoyable day trip. Organized day trips are popular and easy to book through any travel agent in town, or you can plan a journey on your own and travel by bus or rental car. **Puerto Juárez** (✆ **998/877-0618**), just north of Cancún, is the dock for passenger ferries to Isla Mujeres, the least expensive way to travel to Isla. The air-conditioned *Caribbean Express* leaves every half-hour, makes the trip in 20 minutes, has storage space for luggage, and costs about $4. These boats operate daily, starting at 6:30am and ending at 8:30pm. They might leave early if they're full, so arrive ahead of schedule. Pay at the ticket office—or, if the ferry is about to leave, aboard.

Note: Upon arrival by taxi or bus in Puerto Juárez, be wary of pirate "guides" who tell you either that the ferry is canceled or that it's several hours until the next ferry. They'll offer the services of a private *lancha* (small boat) for about $40—and it's nothing but a scam. Small boats are available and, on a co-op basis, charge $15 to $25 one-way, based on the number of passengers. They take about 50 minutes and are not recommended on days with rough seas. Check with the clearly visible ticket office—the only accurate source—for information.

Taxi fares are posted by the street where the taxis park, so be sure to check the rate before agreeing to a taxi for the ride back to Cancún. Rates generally run $12 to $15, depending upon your destination. Moped and bicycle rentals are also readily available as you depart the ferry. This small complex also has public bathrooms, luggage storage, a snack bar, and souvenir shops.

Isla Mujeres is so small that a vehicle isn't necessary, but if you're taking one, you'll use the **Punta Sam** port a little beyond Puerto Juárez. The ferry (40 min.) runs five or six times daily between 8am and 8pm, year-round except in bad weather. Times are generally as follows: Cancún to Isla 8am, 11am, 2:45pm, 5:30pm, and 8:15pm; Isla to Cancún 6:30am, 9:30am, 12:45pm, 4:15pm, and 7:15pm. Always check with the tourist office in Cancún to verify this schedule. Cars should arrive an hour before the ferry departure to register for a place in line and pay the posted fee, which varies depending on the weight and type of vehicle. The sole gas pump in Isla is at the intersection of Avenida Rueda Medina and Calle Abasolo, just northwest of the ferry docks.

There are also ferries to Isla Mujeres from the **Playa Linda,** known as the Embarcadero pier in Cancún, but they're less frequent and more expensive than those from Puerto Juárez. A **Water Taxi** (✆ **998/886-4270** or 998/886-4847; asterix@cablered.net.mx) to Isla Mujeres operates from **Playa Caracol,** between the Fiesta Americana Coral Beach Hotel and the Xcaret terminal on the island, with prices about the same as those from Playa Linda and about four times the cost of the public ferries from Puerto Juárez. Scheduled departures are at 9am, 11am, and 1pm, with returns from Isla Mujeres at noon and 5pm. Adult round-trip fares are $15; kids 3 to 12 pay $7.50; free for children under 3.

To get to Puerto Juárez or Punta Sam from **Cancún,** take any Ruta 8 city bus from Avenida Tulum.

ARRIVING Ferries arrive at the ferry docks (✆ **998/877-0065**) in the center of town. The main road that passes in front is Avenida Rueda Medina. Most hotels are close by. Tricycle taxis are the least expensive and most fun way to get to your hotel; you and your luggage pile in the open carriage compartment, and the driver pedals through the streets. Regular taxis are always lined up in a parking lot to the right of the pier, with their rates posted. If someone on the ferry offers to arrange a taxi for you, politely decline, unless you'd like some help with your luggage down the short pier—it just means an extra, unnecessary tip for your helper.

Isla Mujeres

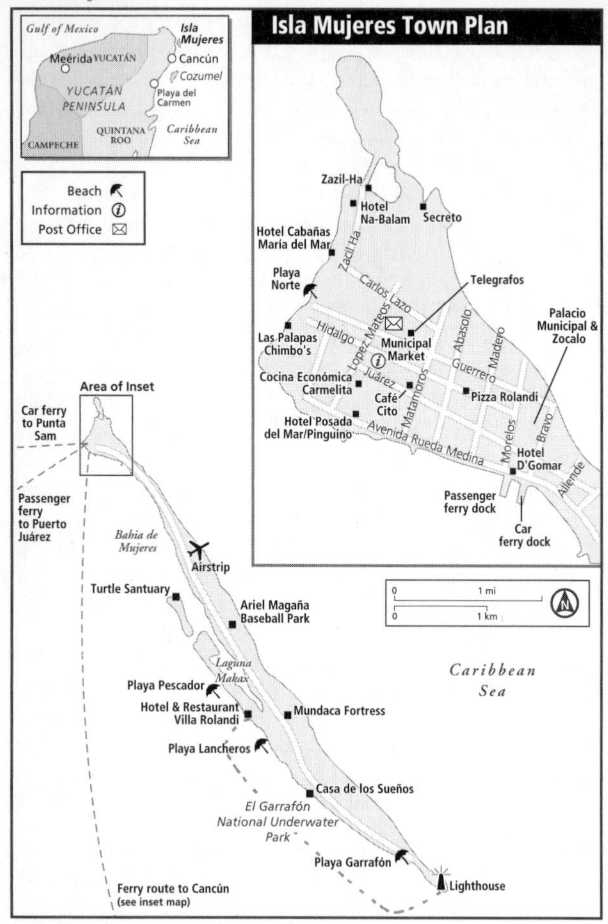

VISITOR INFORMATION The **City Tourist Office** (✆/fax **998/ 877-0767** or 998/877-0307) is at Av. Rueda Medina 130, on your left as you reach the end of the pier. It's open Monday through Friday from 8am to 8pm, Saturday from 8am to 2pm. Also look for *Islander,* a free publication with local information, advertisements, and event listings.

ISLAND LAYOUT Isla Mujeres is about 8km (5 miles) long and 4km (2½ miles) wide, with the town at the northern tip. "Downtown" is a compact 4 blocks by 6 blocks, so it's very easy to get around. The **ferry docks** are at the center of town, within walking distance of most hotels, restaurants, and shops. The street running along the waterfront is **Avenida Rueda Medina,** commonly called the ***malecón*** **(boardwalk).** The **Mercado Municipal (town market)** is by the post office on **Calle Guerrero,** an inland street at the north edge of town, which, like most streets in the town, is unmarked.

GETTING AROUND A popular form of transportation on Isla Mujeres is the electric **golf cart,** available for rent at many hotels for $15 per hour or $45 per day. **El Sol Golf Cart Rental,** Av. Francisco I. Madero 5 (✆ **998/877-0791** or 998/877-0068), will deliver, or you can pick one up. The golf carts don't go more than 32kmph (20 mph), but they're fun. Anyway, you aren't on Isla Mujeres to hurry. Many people enjoy touring the island by ***moto*** **(motorized bike or scooter).** Fully automatic versions are available for around $25 per day or $7 per hour. They come with seats for one person, but some are large enough for two. There's only one main road with a couple of offshoots, so you won't get lost. Be aware that the rental price does not include insurance, and any injury to yourself or the vehicle will come out of your pocket. **Bicycles** are also available for rent at some hotels for $3 per hour or $7 per day, including a basket and a lock.

If you prefer to use a taxi, rates are about $2.50 for trips within the downtown area, or $4.50 for a trip to the southern end of Isla. You can also hire them for about $10 per hour. The number to call for taxis is ✆ **998/877-0066.**

FAST FACTS: Isla Mujeres

Area Code The telephone area code is **998.**

Consumer Protection The local branch of **Profeco** consumer protection agency has a local phone number, ✆ **998/877-0106.**

Currency Exchange Isla Mujeres has numerous *casas de cambio,* or money exchanges, that you can easily spot along the main streets. Most of the hotels listed here change money for their guests, although often at less favorable rates than the commercial enterprises. There is only one bank in Isla, HSBC Bank, across from the ferry docks ✆ **998/877-0104.** It's open Monday through Friday from 8:30am to 6pm, and Saturdays from 9am to 2pm.

Hospital The **Hospital de la Armada** is on Avenida Rueda Medina at Ojón P. Blanco (✆ **998/877-0001**). It's less than a kilometer (½ mile) south of the town center. It will only treat you in an emergency. Otherwise, you're referred to the **Centro de Salud** on Avenida Guerrero, a block before the beginning of the Malecón (✆ **998/877-0117**).

Internet Access Owned by a lifelong resident of Isla, **Cafe Internet Isla Mujeres.com,** Av. Francisco y Madero 17, between Hidalgo and Juaréz streets (✆ **998/877-0272**), offers Internet access for $1.50 per hour from Monday to Sunday 8am to 10pm, and serves complimentary coffee from Veracruz all day.

Pharmacy **Isla Mujeres Farmacia** (✆ **998/877-0178**) has the best selection of prescription and over-the-counter medicines. It's on Calle Benito Juárez, between Morelos and Bravo, across from Rachet & Rome jewelry store.

Post & Telegraph Office The *correo* is at Calle Guerrero 12 (✆ **998/877-0085**), at the corner of López Mateos, near the market. It's open Monday through Friday from 9am to 4pm.

Taxis To call for a taxi, dial ✆ **998/877-0066.**

Telephone Ladatel phones accepting coins and prepaid phone cards are at the plaza and throughout town. **DigaMe,** Avenida Guerrero between Matamoros and Abasolo (✆ **608/467-4202;** info@digame.com), has mobile phone rentals, private voice mail service, and long-distance phone services available.

Tourist Seasons Isla Mujeres's tourist season (when hotel rates are higher) is a bit different from that of other places in Mexico. High season runs December through May, a month longer than in Cancún. Some hotels raise their rates in August, and some raise their rates beginning in mid-November. Low season is from June to mid-November.

BEACHES & OUTDOOR ACTIVITIES

THE BEACHES The most popular beach in town is alternately referred to as **Playa Cocoteros** ("Cocos," for short), or **Playa Norte** ★. The long stretch of beach extends around the northern tip of the island, to your left as you get off the boat. This is a truly splendid beach—a wide stretch of fine white sand and calm, translucent, turquoise-blue water. Topless sunbathing is permitted. The beach is easily reached on foot from the ferry and from all downtown hotels. Watersports equipment, beach umbrellas, and lounge chairs are available for rent. Those in front of restaurants usually cost nothing if you use the restaurant as your headquarters for drinks and food.

El Garrafón Natural Park ★★ (see "Snorkeling," below) is best known as a snorkeling area, but there is a nice stretch of beach on either side of the park. **Playa Lancheros** is on the Caribbean side of Laguna Makax. Local buses go to Lancheros, then turn inland and return downtown. The beach at Playa Lancheros is nice, but the few restaurants there are expensive.

SWIMMING Wide Playa Norte is the best swimming beach, with Playa Lancheros second. There are no lifeguards on duty on Isla Mujeres, which does not use the system of water-safety flags employed in Cancún and Cozumel.

SNORKELING By far the most popular place to snorkel is **El Garrafón Natural Park** ★★. It is at the southern end of the island, where you'll see numerous schools of colorful fish. The well-equipped park has two restaurant-bars, beach chairs, a swimming pool, kayaks, changing rooms, rental lockers, showers, a gift shop, and snack bars. Since late 1999, the same people who manage Xcaret have been operating Garrafón, which is a former public national underwater park. Public facilities have been vastly improved, with new attractions and facilities added each year. Activities at the park include snorkeling and "Snuba" (a tankless version of scuba diving, when you descend while breathing through a long air tube), crystal-clear canoes for viewing underwater life, and a zip-line that takes you over the water. The underwater minisub **Sea Trek** provides a great view of the submarine landscape, and you can keep dry, if that's your preference. On land, they have tanning decks, shaded hammocks, a 12m (40-ft.) climbing tower, and—of course!—a souvenir superstore. Several restaurants and snack bars are available. Admission is $29 for adults, $15 for children (American Express, MasterCard, and Visa are accepted). You can also choose a package ($59) that includes food, beverages, locker rental, and snorkeling gear rental. Day-trip packages from Cancún (✆ **998/884-9422** or 984/875-6000) are also available. Prices start at $22 and include round-trip transportation from the pier on Km 4 outside Cancún. The park is open daily from 9am to 5pm.

Also good for snorkeling is the **Manchones Reef,** off the southeastern coast. The reef is just offshore and accessible by boat.

Another excellent location is around *el faro* (the lighthouse) in the **Bahía de Mujeres** at the southern tip of the island, where the water is about 2m (6 ft.) deep. Boatmen will take you for around $25 per person if you have your own snorkeling equipment or $30 if you use theirs.

DIVING Most of the dive shops on the island offer the same trips for the same prices: One-tank dives cost $55, two-tank dives $70. **Bahía Dive Shop,** Rueda Medina 166, across from the car-ferry dock (✆ **998/877-0340**), is a full-service shop that offers resort and certification classes as well as dive equipment for sale or rent. The shop is open daily from 10am to 7pm, and accepts MasterCard and Visa. Another respected dive shop is **Coral Scuba Center,** at Matamoros 13A and Rueda Medina (✆ **998/877-0061** or 998/877-0763). It's open daily from 8am to 12:30pm and 4 to 10pm.

PADI-certified dive guides and dive instruction is available at **El Garrafón** (✆ **984/875-6000**). Discover Scuba classes are available for $65, with one-tank dives to the Garrafón reef priced at $45, or two-tank dives for $60. Open Water, Advanced, and Rescue PADI certification is also available.

Cuevas de los Tiburones (Caves of the Sleeping Sharks) is Isla's most renowned dive site—but the name is slightly misleading, as shark sightings are rare these days and a storm collapsed the arch featured in a Jacques Cousteau film showing them, but the caves survive. Other dive sites include a **wreck** 15km (9 miles) offshore; **Banderas** reef, between Isla Mujeres and Cancún, where there's always a strong current; **Tabos** reef on the eastern shore; and **Manchones** reef, 1km (½ mile) off the southeastern tip of the island, where the water is 4.5 to 11m (15–35 ft.) deep. **The Cross of the Bay** is close to Manchones reef. A bronze cross, weighing 1 ton and standing 12m (40 ft.) high, was placed in the water between Manchones and Isla in 1994, as a memorial to those who have lost their lives at sea.

FISHING To arrange a day of fishing, ask at the **Sociedad Cooperativa Turística** (the boatmen's cooperative), on Avenida Rueda Medina (no phone), next to Mexico Divers and Las Brisas restaurant, or the travel agency mentioned in "A Visit to Isla Contoy," below. Four to six others can share the cost, which includes lunch and drinks. Captain Tony Martínez (✆ **998/877-0274**) also arranges fishing trips aboard the ***Marinonis,*** with advanced reservations recommended. Year-round you'll find bonito, mackerel, kingfish, and amberjack. Sailfish and sharks (hammerhead, bull, nurse, lemon, and tiger) are in good supply in April and May. In winter, larger grouper and jewfish are prevalent. Four hours of fishing close to shore costs around $110; 8 hours farther out goes for $250. The cooperative is open Monday through Saturday from 8am to 1pm and 5 to 8pm, and Sunday from 7:30 to 10am and 6 to 8pm.

YOGA Increasingly, Isla is becoming known as a great place to combine a relaxing beach vacation with yoga practice and instruction. The trend began at **Hotel Na Balam** ★★ (✆ **998/877-0279** or 998/877-0058; www.nabalam.com), which offers yoga classes under its large poolside *palapa* (an open-sided structure with a thatched roof), complete with yoga mats and props. The classes, which begin at 9am Monday through Friday, are free to guests, $10 per class to visitors. Na Balam is also the site of frequent yoga instruction vacations featuring respected teachers and a more extensive practice schedule; the current schedule of yoga retreats is posted on their website. Local yoga culture extends down the island to **Casa de los Sueños Resort and Spa Zenter** (✆ **998/877-0651;** www.casadelossuenosresort.com), where yoga classes, as well as chi gong and Pilates, are regularly held.

MORE ATTRACTIONS

DOLPHIN DISCOVERY ★★

You can swim with live dolphins (✆ **998/877-0207,** or 998/849-4757 in Cancún; fax 998/849-4751; www.dolphindiscovery.com) in an enclosure at Treasure Island, on the side of Isla Mujeres that faces Cancún. Groups of six people swim with two dolphins and one trainer. Swimmers view an educational video and spend time in the water with the trainer and the dolphins before enjoying 15 minutes of free swimming time with them. Reservations are recommended, and you must arrive an hour before your assigned swimming time, at 9am, 11am, 1pm, or 3pm. The cost is $125 per person, plus $10 if you need round-trip transportation from Cancún. (Please note that swimming with dolphins has its critics and supporters. You may want to visit the Whale and Dolphins Conservation Society's website at www.wdcs.org for more information.)

A TURTLE SANCTUARY ★★

As recently as 20 years ago, fishermen converged on the island nightly from May to September, waiting for the monster-size turtles to lumber ashore to deposit their Ping-Pong-ball-shaped eggs. Totally vulnerable once they begin laying their eggs, and exhausted when they have finished, the turtles were easily captured and slaughtered for their highly prized meat, shell, and eggs. Then a concerned fisherman, Gonzalez Cahle Maldonado, began convincing others to spare at least the eggs, which he protected. It was a start. Following his lead, the fishing secretariat founded the **Centro de Investigaciones** 11 years ago; although the local government provided assistance in the past, now the center relies solely on private donations. Since opening, at least 28,000 turtles have been released, and every year local schoolchildren participate in the event, thus planting the notion of protecting the turtles for a new generation of islanders.

Six species of sea turtles nest on Isla Mujeres. An adult green turtle, the most abundant species, measures 1 to 1.5m (4–5 ft.) in length and can weigh as much as 450 pounds. At the center, visitors walk through the indoor and outdoor turtle pool areas, where the creatures paddle around. The turtles are separated by age, from newly hatched up to 1 year. People who come here usually end up staying at least an hour, especially if they opt for the guided tour, which I recommend. Also here is a small gift shop and snack bar. The sanctuary is on a piece of land separated from the island by Bahía de Mujeres and Laguna Makax, at Carr. Sac Bajo #5; you'll need a taxi to get there. Admission is $3; the shelter is open daily from 9am to 5pm. For more information, call ✆ **998/877-0595.**

SIGHTS OF PUNTA SUR ★★

Also at Punta Sur (the southern point of the island, just inland from **Garrafón National Park** [✆ **998/877-1100;** www.garrafon.com]) and part of the Park, is Isla's newest attraction, the **Panoramic Tower.** At 50m (225 ft.) high, the tower offers visitors a birds' eye view of the entire island. The tower holds 20 visitors at a time, and rotates for ten minutes while you can snap photos or simply enjoy the scenery. Entry fee is $5, a professional photo of you at the tower (touch-ups are included!) is $10, and package prices are available.

Next to the tower you'll find **Sculptured Spaces,** an impressive and extensive garden of large sculptures donated to Isla Mujeres by internationally renowned sculptors as part of the 2001 First International Sculpture Exhibition. Among Mexican sculptors represented are works by Jose Luis Cuevas and Vladimir Cora.

Nearby is the **Caribbean Village,** with narrow lanes of colorful clapboard buildings that house cafes and shops displaying folkloric art. Plan to have lunch or a snack here at the kiosk and stroll around, before heading on to the lighthouse and Mayan ruins.

Also at this southern point of the island, and part of the ruins is **Cliff of the Dawn,** the southeastern-most point of Mexico. Services are available from 7am to 8pm, but you can enter at any time; if you make it there early enough to see the sun rise, you can claim you were the first person in Mexico that day to be touched by the sun!

A MAYA RUIN ★★

Just beyond the lighthouse, at the southern end of the island, are the strikingly beautiful remains of a small Maya temple, believed to have been built in homage to the moon and fertility goddess Ixchel. The location, on a lofty bluff overlooking the sea, is worth seeing and makes a great place for photos. It is believed that Maya women traveled here on annual pilgrimages to seek Ixchel's blessings of fertility. If you're at El Garrafón park and want to walk, it's not too far. Turn right from El Garrafón. When you see the lighthouse, turn toward it down the rocky path.

A PIRATE'S FORTRESS

The Fortress of Mundaca is about 4km (2½ miles) in the same direction as El Garrafón, less than a kilometer (about ½ mile) to the left. A slave trader who claimed to have been the pirate Mundaca Marecheaga built the fortress. In the early 19th century, he arrived at Isla Mujeres and set up a blissful paradise, while making money selling slaves to Cuba and Belize. According to island lore, he decided to settle down and build this hacienda after being captivated by the charms of an island girl. However, she reputedly spurned his affections and married another islander, leaving him heartbroken and alone on Isla Mujeres. Admission is $2; the fortress is open daily from 10am to 6pm.

A VISIT TO ISLA CONTOY ★

If possible, visit this pristine uninhabited island, which became a national wildlife reserve in 1981. Isla Contoy is 30km (20 miles) by boat from Isla Mujeres. Lush vegetation covers the oddly shaped island, which is 6km (3¾ miles) long and harbors 70 species of birds as well as a host of marine and animal life. Bird species that nest on the island include pelicans, brown boobies, frigates, egrets, terns, and cormorants. Flocks of flamingos arrive in April. June, July, and August are good months to spot turtles burying their eggs in the sand at night. Most excursions troll for fish (which will be your lunch), anchor en route for a snorkeling expedition, skirt the island at a leisurely pace for close viewing of the birds without disturbing the habitat, and then pull ashore. While the captain prepares lunch, visitors can swim, sun, follow the nature trails, and visit the fine nature museum, which has bathroom facilities. The trip from Isla

Mujeres takes about 45 minutes each way and can be longer if the waves are choppy. Because of the tight-knit boatmen's cooperative, prices for this excursion are the same everywhere: $40. You can buy a ticket at the **Sociedad Cooperativa Turística** on Avenida Rueda Medina, next to Mexico Divers and Las Brisas restaurant (no phone), or at one of several **travel agencies,** such as **La Isleña,** on Morelos between Medina and Juárez (© **998/877-0578**). La Isleña is open daily from 7:30am to 9:30pm and is a good source for tourist information. Isla Contoy trips leave at 8:30am and return around 4pm. The price (cash only) is $37 for adults, $18 for children. Boat captains should respect the cooperative's regulations regarding ecological sensitivity, and boat safety, including the availability of life jackets for everyone on board. Snorkeling equipment is usually included in the price, but double-check that before heading out. On the island, there is a small government museum with bathroom facilities.

SHOPPING

Shopping is a casual activity here. There are only a few shops of any sophistication. Shop owners will bombard you, especially on Avenida Hidalgo, selling Saltillo rugs, onyx, silver, Guatemalan clothing, blown glassware, masks, folk art, beach paraphernalia, and T-shirts in abundance. Prices are lower than in Cancún or Cozumel, but with such overeager sellers, bargaining is necessary.

The one treasure you're likely to take back is a piece of fine jewelry—Isla is known for its excellent, duty-free prices on gemstones and handcrafted work made to order. Diamonds, emeralds, sapphires, and rubies can be purchased as loose stones and then mounted while you're off exploring. The superbly crafted gold, silver, and gems are available at very competitive prices in the workshops near the central plaza. The stones are also available in the rough. **Rachet & Rome** (© **998/877-0331**) located at the corner of Morelos and Juárez streets, is the grandest store, with a broad selection of jewelry at competitive prices. It's open daily from 9:30am to 5pm and accepts all major credit cards.

WHERE TO STAY

You'll find plenty of hotels in all price ranges on Isla Mujeres. Rates peak during high season, which is the most expensive and most crowded time to go. Elizabeth Wenger of **Four Seasons Travel** in Montello, Wisconsin (© **800/552-4550**), specializes in Mexico travel and books a lot of hotels in Isla Mujeres. Her service is invaluable in the high season. Those interested in private home rentals or longer-term stays can contact **Mundaca Travel and Real Estate** in Isla Mujeres (✆ **998/877-0025;** fax 998/877-0076; www.mundacar travel.com).

VERY EXPENSIVE

Casa de los Sueños Resort and Spa Zenter ★★★ This "house of dreams" is easily Isla Mujeres's most intimate, sophisticated, and relaxing property. Though it was originally built as a private residence, it became an upscale, adults-only B&B in early 1998 and now caters to guests looking for a rejuvenating experience, with its adjoining "Zenter" offering spa services and yoga classes. Its location on the southern end of the island, adjacent to El Garrafón National Park, also makes it ideal for snorkeling and diving enthusiasts. The captivating design features vivid sherbet-colored walls and a sculpted architecture. There's a large, open interior courtyard; tropical gardens; a sunken living area (with wireless Internet access); and an infinity pool. All rooms have balconies or terraces and face west, offering stunning views.

Carretera Garrafón s/n, 77400 Isla Mujeres, Q. Roo. ✆ **998/877-0651** or 998/877-0369. Fax 998/877-0708. www.casadelossuenosresort.com. 7 units. High season $300–$450 double; low season $240–$360 double. Rates include continental breakfast. MC, V. No children. **Amenities:** Restaurant; breakfast delivery; infinity pool; spa, yoga center, and open-air massage area; 24-hr. room service. *In room:* TV/VCR, hair dryer, iron, safe.

Hotel Villa Rolandi Gourmet & Beach Club ★★★ This hotel has become a great addition to Isla's options for guests who enjoy its tranquillity—but also like being pampered. The Mediterranean-style rooms offer every conceivable amenity, and the hotel has its own small, private beach in a sheltered cove. Each of the oversize suites has an ocean view and a large terrace or balcony with a full-size private whirlpool. TVs offer satellite music and movies, and rooms all have a sophisticated in-room sound system. A recessed seating area extends out to the balcony or terrace.

Fracc. Lagunamar SM 7 Mza. 75 L 15 and 16, 77400 Isla Mujeres, Q. Roo. ✆ **998/877-0700.** Fax 998/877-0100. www.villarolandi.com. 20 units. High season $350–$420 double; low season $290–$350 double. Rates include round-trip transportation from Playa Linda in Cancún aboard private catamaran yacht; continental breakfast; and a la carte lunch or dinner in the on-site restaurant. AE, MC, V. Children under 14 not accepted. **Amenities:** Restaurant (see "Where to Dine," below); breakfast delivery; infinity pool w/waterfall; small fitness room w/basic equipment and open-air massage area; concierge; tour desk; 24-hr. room service. *In room:* TV/VCR, dataport, minibar, hair dryer, iron, safe.

EXPENSIVE

Hotel Na Balam ★★ *Finds* Na Balam is known as a haven for yoga students. This popular, two-story hotel near the end of Playa Norte has comfortable rooms on a quiet, ideally located portion of the beach. Rooms are in three sections; some face the beach, and others are across the street in a garden setting with a swimming pool. All rooms have a terrace or balcony with hammocks. Each spacious suite contains a king or two double beds, a seating area, and folk-art decorations. Two were redecorated in 2004 in a more sophisticated style, and with small pools with hydromassage situated under coconut trees.

Zazil Ha 118, 77400 Isla Mujeres, Q. Roo. ✆ **998/877-0279.** Fax 998/877-0446. www.nabalam.com. 31 units. High season $162–$270 suite; low season $121–$200 suite. Ask about weekly and monthly rates. AE, MC, V. **Amenities:** Restaurant; 2 bars; swimming pool; diving and snorkeling trips available; mopeds, golf carts, and bikes for rent; game room w/TV, VCR, and Ping-Pong tables; salon; in-room massage; babysitting; laundry service; library; Internet access; yoga classes. *In room:* A/C, fan.

Secreto ★★ *Finds* This new boutique hotel looks like a Hamptons beach house, but it is one of the best B&B values in the Caribbean. What sets Secreto apart—aside from the stunning setting and outstanding value—is the exemplary service. The sophisticated, romantic property has nine suites that overlook a central pool area to the private beach beyond. Located on the northern end of the island, Secreto is within walking distance of town, yet feels removed enough to make for an idyllic, peaceful retreat. All rooms have private verandas with comfortable seating, ideal for ocean-gazing beyond Halfmoon Beach, and are accented with original artwork.

Sección Rocas, Lote 1, 77400 Isla Mujeres, Q. Roo. ✆ **877/278-8018** in the U.S., or 998/877-1039. Fax 998/877-1048. www.hotelsecreto.com. 9 units. High season $183–$250 double; low season $167–$230 double. Extra person $15. 1 child under 5 stays free in parent's room. Rates include continental breakfast. MC, V. **Amenities:** Pool; private cove beach; tours, diving and snorkeling available; dinner delivery from Rolandi's restaurant available. *In room:* A/C, TV, fridge, safe, bathrobes, CD player.

MODERATE

Hotel Cabañas María del Mar ★ A good choice for simple beach accommodations, the Cabañas María del Mar is on the popular Playa Norte. The older two-story section behind the reception area and beyond the garden offers nicely outfitted rooms facing the beach. All have two single or double beds, refrigerators, and ocean-view balconies strung with hammocks. Eleven single-story cabañas closer to the reception area are decorated in a rustic Mexican style. The third section, **El Castillo** is across the street. It contains all "deluxe" rooms, but some are larger than others; the five rooms on the ground floor have large patios. Upstairs rooms have small balconies. Rooms were remodeled in 2004. There's a small pool in the garden.

Av. Arq. Carlos Lazo 1 (on Playa Norte, ½ block from the Hotel Na Balam), 77400 Isla Mujeres, Q. Roo. ✆ **800/223-5695** in the U.S., or 998/877-0179. Fax 998/877-0213. 73 units. High season $109–$123 double; low season $70–$111 double. MC, V. From the pier, walk left 1 block and turn right on Matamoros. After 4 blocks, turn left on Lazo (the last street); hotel is at end of block. **Amenities:** Pool; bus for tours and boat for rent; golf cart and *moto* rentals. *In room:* Fridge in cabañas.

INEXPENSIVE

Hotel D'Gomar *Value* This hotel is known for comfort at reasonable prices. You can hardly beat the value for basic accommodations, which are regularly updated. Rooms have two double beds and a wall of windows offers great breezes and views. The higher prices are for air-conditioning, which is hardly needed with the breezes and ceiling fans. The only drawback is that there are five stories and no elevator. But it's conveniently located cater-cornered (look right) from the ferry pier, with exceptional rooftop views. The name of the hotel is the most visible sign on the "skyline."

Rueda Medina 150, 77400 Isla Mujeres, Q. Roo. ✆ **998/877-0541.** 16 units. High season $40 double; low season $35 double. No credit cards. *In room:* Fan.

Hotel Posada del Mar *Kids* Simply furnished, quiet, and comfortable, this long-established hotel faces the water and a wide beach 3 blocks north of the ferry pier. It has one of the few swimming pools on the island. This is probably the best choice in Isla for families. The ample rooms are in a three-story building or one-story bungalow units. For the spaciousness of the rooms and the location, this is among the best values on the island and is very popular with readers, though I consistently find the staff to be the least gracious on the island. A great, casual *palapa*-style bar and a lovely pool are on the back lawn along with hammocks.

Av. Rueda Medina 15 A, 77400 Isla Mujeres, Q. Roo. ✆ **800/544-3005** in the U.S., or 998/877-0044. Fax 998/877-0266. www.posadadelmar.com. 62 units. High season $67–$77 double; low season $40–$45 double. Children under 12 stay free in parent's room. AE, MC, V. From the pier, go left for 4 blocks; hotel is on the right. **Amenities:** Restaurant/bar; pool. *In room:* A/C, TV, fan.

WHERE TO DINE

At the **Municipal Market,** next to the telegraph office and post office on Avenida Guerrero, obliging, hardworking women operate several little food stands. At the **Panadería La Reyna** (no phone), at Madero and Juárez, you can pick up inexpensive sweet bread, muffins, cookies, and yogurt. It's open Monday through Saturday from 7am to 9:30pm.

Cocina económica (literally, "economic kitchen") restaurants usually aim at the local population. These are great places to find good food at rock-bottom prices, and especially so on Isla Mujeres, where you'll find several, most of which feature delicious regional specialties. But be aware that the hygiene is not what you'll find at more established restaurants, so you're dining at your own risk.

EXPENSIVE

Casa Rolandi ★ ITALIAN/SEAFOOD The gourmet Casa Rolandi restaurant and bar has become Isla's favored fine-dining experience. It boasts a view of the Caribbean and the most sophisticated menu in the area. There's a colorful main dining area as well as more casual, open-air terrace seating for drinks or light snacks. The food is the most notable on the island, but the overall experience falls short—the lights are a bit too bright and the music a bit too close to what you'd hear on an elevator. Along with seafood and northern Italian specialties, the famed wood-burning-oven pizzas are a good bet. Careful—the wood-oven-baked bread, which arrives looking like a puffer fish, is so divine that you're likely to fill up on it. This is a great place to enjoy the sunset, and it offers a selection of more than 80 premium tequilas.

On the pier of Villa Rolandi, Lagunamar SM 7. ✆ **998/877-0700.** Main courses $8–$35. AE, MC, V. Daily 11am–11pm.

MODERATE

Las Palapas Chimbo's ★ SEAFOOD If you're looking for a beachside *palapa*-covered restaurant where you can wiggle your toes in the sand while relishing fresh seafood, this is the best of them. It's the locals' favorite on Playa Norte. Try the delicious fried whole fish, which comes with rice, beans, and tortillas. You'll notice a bandstand and dance floor in the middle of the restaurant, and sex-hunk posters all over the ceiling—that is, when you aren't gazing at the beach and the Caribbean. Chimbo's becomes a lively bar and dance club at night, drawing a crowd of drinkers and dancers.

Norte Beach. No phone. Sandwiches and fruit $2.50–$4.50; seafood $6–$9. No credit cards. Daily 8am–midnight. From the pier, walk left to the end of the *malecón,* then right onto the Playa Norte; it's about ½ block on the right.

Pinguino MEXICAN/SEAFOOD The best seats on the waterfront are on the deck of this restaurant and bar, especially in late evening, when islanders and tourists arrive to dance and party. This is the place to feast on sublimely fresh lobster—you'll get a large, beautifully presented lobster tail with a choice of butter, garlic, and secret sauces. The grilled seafood platter is spectacular, and fajitas and barbecued ribs are also popular. Breakfasts include fresh fruit, yogurt, and granola, or sizable platters of eggs, served with homemade wheat bread. Pinguino also has nonsmoking areas.

In front of the Hotel Posada del Mar (3 blocks west of the ferry pier), Av. Rueda Medina 15. ✆ **998/877-0044,** ext. 157. Main courses $4–$7; daily special $7. AE, MC, V. Daily 7am–11pm; bar closes at midnight.

Pizza Rolandi ★★ ITALIAN/SEAFOOD You're bound to dine at least once at Rolandi's, which is practically an Isla institution. The plate-size pizzas and calzones feature exotic ingredients—including lobster, black mushrooms, pineapple, and Roquefort cheese—as well as more traditional tomatoes, olives, basil, and salami. A wood-burning oven provides the signature flavor of the pizzas, as well as baked chicken, roast beef, and mixed seafood casserole with lobster. The extensive menu also offers a selection of salads and light appetizers, as well as an ample array of pasta dishes, steaks, fish, and scrumptious desserts. The setting is the open courtyard of the Hotel Belmar, with a porch overlooking the action on Avenida Hidalgo.

Av. Hidalgo 10 (3½ blocks inland from the pier, between Madero and Abasolo). ✆ **998/877-0430,** ext. 18. Main courses $3.70–$13. AE, MC, V. Daily 11am–11:30pm.

Zazil Ha ★★ CARIBBEAN/INTERNATIONAL Here you can enjoy some of the island's best food while sitting at tables on the sand among palms and gardens. The food—terrific pasta with garlic, shrimp in tequila sauce, fajitas, seafood pasta, and delicious *mole* enchiladas—enhances the serene environment. Caribbean specialties include cracked conch, coconut sailfish, jerk chicken, and stuffed squid. A selection of fresh juices complements the vegetarian menu, and there's even a special menu for those participating in yoga retreats. Between the set meal times, you can order all sorts of enticing food, such as vegetable and fruit drinks, tacos and sandwiches, ceviche, and terrific nachos. It's likely you'll stake this place out for several meals.

At the Hotel Na Balam (at the end of Playa Norte, almost at the end of Calle Zazil Ha). ✆ **998/877-0279.** Fax 998/877-0446. Main courses $8.50–$16. AE, MC, V. Daily 7:30–10:30am, 12:30–3:30pm, and 6:30–11pm.

INEXPENSIVE

Café Cito ★ CREPES/ICE CREAM/COFFEE/FRUIT DRINKS Sabina and Luis Rivera own this cute, Caribbean-blue corner restaurant where you can begin the day with flavorful coffee and a croissant and cream cheese, or end it with a hot-fudge sundae. Terrific crepes come with yogurt, ice cream, fresh fruit, or chocolate sauce, as well as ham and cheese. The two-page ice cream menu satisfies almost any craving, even one for waffles with ice cream and fruit. The three-course fixed-price dinner includes soup, a main course (such as fish or curried shrimp with rice and salad), and dessert.

Calle Matamoros 42, at Juárez (4 blocks from the pier). ✆ **998/877-1470.** Crepes $2–$4.50; breakfast $2.50–$4.50; sandwiches $2.80–$2.90. No credit cards. Year-round daily 8am–2pm; high season Fri–Wed 5:30–10:30 or 11:30pm.

Cocina Económica Carmelita MEXICAN/HOME COOKING Few tourists find their way to this tiny restaurant, but locals know they can get a filling, inexpensive, home-cooked meal. Carmelita prepares food in the back kitchen, and her husband serves it at the three cloth-covered tables in the front room of their home. Two or three *comida corridas* are available each day until they run out. They begin with the soup of the day and include *agua fresca* (a fruit water drink). Common selections include *paella, cochinita pibil* (pork with *achiote,* sour orange, and spices), and fish-stuffed chiles. Menu specialties include chicken in *mole* sauce, pork cutlet in a spicy sauce, and breaded shrimp. For fancier tastes, the least expensive lobster in town—served grilled or in a garlic sauce—costs $13 for an ample portion.

Calle Juárez 14 (2 blocks from the pier, between Bravo and Allende). No phone. Main dishes $4–$6; daily lunch special $4. No credit cards. Year-round Mon–Sat 12:30–3pm; Dec–Mar Mon–Sat 4–8pm.

2 Eco Theme Parks & Reserves

The popularity of Xcaret and Xel-Ha has inspired entrepreneurs to ride the wave of interest in ecological and adventure theme parks. Be aware that "theme park" is the more pertinent part of the phrase. The newer parks of Aktun Chen and Tres Ríos are—so far—less commercial and more focused on nature than their predecessors. Included here are several true reserves, which have less in the way of facilities but offer an authentic encounter with the natural beauty of the region.

AKTUN CHEN ★

This park, consisting of a spectacular 5,000-year-old grotto and an abundance of wildlife, is the first above-the-ground cave system in the Yucatán to be open to the public. The name means "cave with an underground river inside," and the main cave (of three) is more than 550m (1,800 ft.) long, with a magnificent vault. Discreet illumination and easy walking paths make visiting the caves comfortable, without appearing to alter them much from their natural state. The caves contain thousands of stalactites, stalagmites, and sculpted rock formations, along with a 12m-deep (40-ft.) *cenote* with clear blue water. Aktun Chen was once underwater, and fossilized shells and fish embedded in the limestone are visible as you walk along the paths. Knowledgeable guides provide explanations of what you see and offer mini–history lessons in the Maya's association with these caves. Tours have no set times—guides are available to take you when you arrive—and the maximum group size is 20. Surrounding the caves, nature trails wind throughout the 400-hectare (990-acre) park, where spottings of deer, spider monkeys, iguanas, and wild turkeys are common. A small informal restaurant and gift shop are also on-site.

It's easy to travel by yourself to Aktun Chen (✆ **998/892-0662** or 998/850-4190; www.aktunchen.com); from Cancún, go south along Highway 307, the road to Tulum. Just past the turnoff for Akumal, a sign on the right side of the highway indicates the turnoff to Aktun-Chen, and from there it's a 3km (2-mile) drive west along a smooth but unpaved road. Travel time from Cancún is about an hour. The park is open daily from 9am to 5pm; the last tour departs at 4pm. The entry fee of $19 for adults, $10 for children includes the services of a guide.

EL EDEN RESERVA ECOLOGICA

Established in 1990, this is a privately owned 200,000-hectare (500,000-acre) reserve dedicated to research for biological conservation in Mexico. It takes around 2 hours to reach the center of this reserve deep in the jungle, yet it's only 48km (30 miles) northwest of Cancún. It's intended as an overnight (or longer) excursion for people who want to know more about the biological diversity of the peninsula.

Within the reserve, or near it, are marine grasslands, mangrove swamps, rainforests, savannas, wetlands, and sand dunes, as well as evidence of archaeological sites and at least 205 species of birds, plus orchids, bromeliads, and cacti. Among the local animals are the spider monkey, jaguar, cougar, deer, and ocelot. The "ecoscientific" tours include naturalist-led birding, animal tracking, stargazing, spotlight surveys for nocturnal wildlife, and exploration of *cenotes* and Maya ruins. Comfortable, basic accommodations are provided. Tours include transportation from Cancún, 1 or 2 nights of accommodation at La Savanna Research Station, meals, nightly cocktails, guided nature walks, and tours. The tours cost $235 to $380, depending on the length of stay, plus $95 per extra night. American Express is accepted. Contact **Ecocolors,** Camarón 32 SM 27 (✆ **998/884-3667;** fax 998/884-9580; www.ecotravelmexico.com), which specializes in ecologically oriented tours around the Cancún area.

TRES RIOS ★

This ecoadventure park 25 minutes south of Cancún is actually a nature reserve on more than 60 hectares (150 acres) of land. Tres Ríos (✆ **998/887-8077** in Cancún; www.tres-rios.com) offers guests a beautiful natural area for kayaking, canoeing, snorkeling, horseback riding, or biking along jungle trails. It's definitely less commercial than the other eco-theme parks and is essentially just a great natural area for participating in these activities. The entrance fee—$22 for adults, $19 for children—includes canoe trips; the use of bikes, kayaks, and snorkeling equipment; and the use of hammocks and beach chairs once you tire yourself out. Extra charges apply for scuba diving, horseback riding, and other extended, guided tours through the preserve and its estuary. You can also opt for an all-inclusive package that covers admission, diving, horseback riding, and all food and beverages. It costs $75 per adult, $62 for children under 12, and reservations are required. Tres Ríos also has bathroom facilities, showers, and a convenience store. Most Cancún travel agencies sell a half-day Kayak Express tour to Tres Ríos. Priced at $48, it includes admission and activities, plus round-trip transportation, lunch, and two nonalcoholic drinks. The park is open daily from 9am to 5pm.

XCARET: A DEVELOPED NATURE PARK

Eighty kilometers (50 miles) south of Cancún and 10km (6½ miles) south of Playa del Carmen is the turnoff to **Xcaret** (pronounced Ish-cah-*ret*), an ecological and archaeological theme park that is one of the area's most popular tourist attractions. It's the closest thing to Disneyland that you'll find in Mexico, with myriad attractions in one location, most of them participatory. Signs throughout Cancún advertise Xcaret, which has its own bus terminal to take tourists there at regular intervals. Plan to spend a full day.

Xcaret may celebrate Mother Nature, but its builders rearranged quite a bit of her handiwork in completing it. If you're looking for a place to escape the commercialism of Cancún, this may not be it; it's relatively expensive and may be very crowded, diminishing the advertised "natural" experience. Children love it, however, and the jungle setting and palm-lined beaches are beautiful. Once past the entrance booths (built to resemble small Maya temples) you'll find pathways that meander around **bathing coves,** the **snorkeling lagoon,** and the remains of a group of real **Maya temples.** You'll have access to **swimming beaches;** limestone tunnels to snorkel through; marked palm-lined pathways; a **wild-bird breeding aviary; a *charro* exhibition; horseback riding; scuba diving; a botanical garden and nursery; a sea turtle nursery** that releases the turtles after their first year; a pavilion showcasing **regional butterflies;** a tropical **aquarium** where visitors can touch underwater creatures such as manta rays, starfish, and octopi; and a "Dolphinarium," where visitors (on a first-come, first-served basis) can swim with the dolphins for an extra charge of $90.

Another attraction at Xcaret is a replica of the ancient Maya game **pok-ta-pok,** where six "warriors" bounce around a 9-pound ball with their hips. The Seawalker is a watersport designed for non-swimmers. By donning a special suit and helmet with a connected air pump, you can walk on the ocean floor or examine a coral reef in a small bay.

There is also a visitor center with lockers, first aid, and gifts. Visitors aren't allowed to bring in food or drinks, so you're limited to the rather expensive on-site restaurants. No personal radios are allowed, and you must remove all suntan lotion if you swim in the lagoon (to avoid poisoning the habitat).

Xcaret is open Monday through Saturday from 8:30am to 9pm, Sunday from 8:30am to 5:30pm. The admission price of $49 per person entitles you to all the facilities—boats, life jackets, and snorkeling equipment—for the underwater tunnel and lagoon, and lounge chairs and other facilities. Other attractions—such as snorkeling ($32), horseback riding ($49), scuba diving ($55 for certified divers, $75 for a resort course), and the dolphin swim ($90)—cost extra. There may be more visitors than equipment (such as beach chairs), so bring a beach towel and your own snorkeling gear. Travel agencies in Cancún offer day trips to Xcaret that include transportation, admission, and a guide. They depart at 8am, return at 6pm, and cost $75 for adults and $55 for children. The "Xcaret Day and Night" package includes round-trip transportation from Cancún, a *charreada* (equestrian arts) festival, lighted pathways to Maya ruins, dinner, and a folkloric show. It's $89 for adults, $40 for children age 5 to 11, free for children under 5. Buses leave the terminal at 8:15 and 10:35am daily, with the "Day and Night" tour returning at 9:30pm. You can also buy tickets to the park at the **Xcaret Terminal** (✆ **998/883-3143**), next to the Fiesta Americana Grand Coral Beach hotel on Cancún Island.

XEL-HA ★★

The ecopark at Xel-Ha (✆ **998/884-9422;** www.xelha.com), 13km (8 miles) south of Akumal, attracts throngs of snorkelers and divers with its warm waters and brilliant fish. The beautiful, calm cove is a perfect place to bring kids for their first snorkeling experience.

The centerpiece of Xel-Ha (Shell-*hah*) is a large, beautiful **lagoon** where freshwater and saltwater meet. You can swim, float, and snorkel in beautifully clear water surrounded by jungle. A small train takes guests upriver to a drop-off point. There, you can store all your clothes and gear in a locked sack that is taken down to the locker rooms in the main part of the building. The water moves calmly toward the sea, and you can float along with it. Snorkeling here offers a higher comfort level than the open sea—there are no waves and currents to pull you about, but there are a lot of fish of several species, including rays.

Inside the park, you can rent snorkeling equipment and an underwater camera. Platforms allow nonsnorkelers to view the fish. Another way to view fish is to use the park's "snuba" gear—a contraption that allows you to breathe air through 6m (20-ft.) tubes connected to scuba tanks floating on the surface. It frees you of the cumbersome tank while allowing you to stay down without having to hold your breath. Rental costs $42 for approximately an hour. Like snuba but more involved is "sea-trek," a device consisting of an elaborate plastic helmet with air hoses. It allows you to walk around on the bottom breathing normally and perhaps participate in feeding the park's stingrays. Another attraction is swimming with dolphins. A 1-hour swim costs $115; a 15-minute program costs $40. Make reservations (✆ **998/887-6840**) at least 24 hours in advance for one of the four daily sessions. Also on site are a **plant nursery,** an **apiary** for the local, stingless Maya bees, and a lovely path through the **tropical forest** bordering the lagoon.

Xel-Ha is open daily from 8:30am to 5pm. Parking is free. For the basic package, adult admission is $36 on weekdays, $28 on weekends; admission for children ages 5 to 11 is $18 on weekdays, $13 on weekends; children under 5 enter free. Admission includes use of inner tubes, life vest, and shuttle train to the river, and the use of changing rooms and showers. An all-inclusive option includes snorkeling equipment rental, locker rental, towels, food, and beverages. Adults can visit all week long for $67, and children visit for $33. The park has five restaurants, two ice cream shops, and a store. It accepts American Express, MasterCard, and Visa, and has an ATM.

Signs clearly mark the turnoff to Xel-Ha. Xel-Ha is close to the ruins of Tulum. A popular day tour from Cancún or Playa combines the two. If you're traveling on your own, the best time to enjoy Xel-Ha without the crowds is during the weekend from 9am to 2pm.

Just south of the Xel-Ha turnoff on the west side of Highway 307, don't miss the ruins of **ancient Xel-Ha** ★. You'll likely be the only one there as you walk over limestone rocks and through the tangle of trees, vines, and palms. There is a huge, deep, dark *cenote* to one side, a temple palace with tumbled-down columns, stone statues of jaguars, and a conserved temple group. A covered *palapa* on one pyramid guards a partially preserved mural. Admission is $3.50.

About 2km (1 mile) south of Xel-Ha are the **Hidden Worlds Cenotes** ★★★ (✆ **984/877-8535**; www.hiddenworlds.com.mx), which offer an excellent opportunity to snorkel or dive in a couple of nearby caverns. The caverns are part of a vast network that makes up a single underground river system. The water is crystalline (and a bit cold) and the rock formations impressive. These caverns were filmed for the IMAX production *Journey into Amazing Caves.* The people running the show are resourceful. When I was last there, they were putting together a new way to view the caverns using 90 to 120m (300–400 ft.) of submerged half-sections of tubes that will create a long air pocket for viewing the cavern. This is their own invention (which they've dubbed "tube-a-scuba"), and I'm curious

---

Tips **Visiting Xel-Ha & Tulum**

Xel-Ha is close to Tulum (discussed in chapter 5) and makes a good place for a dip when you've finished climbing those Maya ruins. You can even make the 13km (8-mile) hop north from Tulum to Xel-Ha by public bus. When you get off at the junction for Tulum, ask the restaurant owner when the next buses come by; otherwise, you may have to wait as long as 2 hours on the highway.

---

to see how it will work. The snorkel tour costs $40 and takes you to different caverns. The main form of transportation is "jungle mobile," with a guide who throws in tidbits of information and lore about the jungle plant life that you see. There is some walking involved, so take shoes or sandals. I've toured several caverns, but floating through one gave me an entirely different perspective.

3 Exploring the Punta Allen Peninsula

If you've been captured by an adventurous spirit and have an excessively sanguine opinion of your rental car, you might want to take a trip down the Punta Allen Peninsula, especially if your interests lie in fly-fishing, birding, or simply exploring new country. The far end of the peninsula is only 50km (30 miles) away, but it can be a very slow trip (up to 3 hr., depending on the condition of the road). Not far from the last cabaña hotel is the entrance to the 500,000-hectare (1.3-million-acre) **Sian Ka'an Biosphere Reserve** (see below). Halfway down the peninsula, at Boca Paila, a bridge crosses to the lower peninsula, where the Boca Paila Fishing Lodge is. On your right is a large lagoon. Another 25km (15 miles) gets you to the village of **Punta Allen,** where you can arrange a birding expedition (available June–Aug, with July being best) or a boat trip (see the entry for Cuzan Guest House in "Where to Stay," below).

THE SIAN KA'AN BIOSPHERE RESERVE ★

Down the peninsula a few miles south of the Tulum ruins, you'll pass the guardhouse of the Sian Ka'an Biosphere Reserve. The reserve is a tract of 500,000 hectares (1.3 million acres) set aside in 1986 to preserve tropical forests, savannas, mangroves, coastal and marine habitats, and 110km (70 miles) of coastal reefs. The area is home to jaguars, pumas, ocelots, margays, jaguarundis, spider and howler monkeys, tapirs, white-lipped and collared peccaries, manatees, brocket and white-tailed deer, crocodiles, and green, loggerhead, hawksbill, and leatherback sea turtles. It also protects 366 species of birds—you might catch a glimpse of an ocellated turkey, a great curassow, a brilliantly colored parrot, a toucan or trogon, a white ibis, a roseate spoonbill, a jabiru (or wood stork), a flamingo, or one of 15 species of herons, egrets, and bitterns.

The park has three parts: a "core zone" restricted to research; a "buffer zone," to which visitors and families already living there have restricted use; and a "cooperation zone," which is outside the reserve but vital to its preservation. Driving south from Tulum on Highway 307, everything on the left side of the highway is part of the reserve. Most tours enter the biopreserve on this side at the community of Muyil where there are canals built by the Maya that lead to a lagoon. At least 22 archaeological sites have been charted within Sian Ka'an.

The Friends of Sian Ka'an, a nonprofit group based in Cancún, offers biologist-escorted day trips, weather permitting, from the **Cabañas Ana y José** (www.anayjose.com), just south of the Tulum ruins. They cost $68 per person in a company vehicle, or $58 per person if you drive yourself. The price includes chips and soft drinks, round-trip van transportation to the reserve, a guided boat and birding trip through one of the reserve's lagoons, and use of binoculars. Tours can accommodate up to 18 people. Trips start from the Cabañas Monday through Saturday at 9am and return there around 3pm. For reservations, contact **Amigos de Sian Ka'an,** Crepúsculo 18, and Amanecer, Supermanzana 44, Manzana 13 Residencial Alborada, Cancún (✆ **998/848-2136,** 998/848-1618, or 998/848-1593; fax 998/848-1618; sian@cancun.com.mx). Office hours are from 9am to 5pm.

Visitors can arrange day trips in Tulum at **Sian Ka'an Tours** (✆ **984/871-2363;** siankaan_tours@hotmail.com), on the east side of the road, .3km (less than ¼ mile) south of the highway intersection, next to Los Tucanes restaurant.

WHERE TO STAY

The peninsula offers simple but comfortable lodgings. One or two have electricity for a few hours in the evening, but it goes off around 10pm. Halfway down the peninsula, the **Boca Paila Fishing Lodge** (✆ **800/245-1950,** or 412/935-1577 in the U.S.) specializes in hosting fly-fishers. Its weeklong packages include everything, even the boat and guide.

Between Boca Paila and Punta Allen are a couple of small, comfortable hotels run by Americans, perfect for getting away from it all. One is **Rancho Sol Caribe** (no phone; www.cancun.com), which has only two or three rooms on a private beach. Punta Allen is a lobstering and fishing village on a palm-studded beach. Isolated and rustic, it's the most laid-back end of the line you'll find for a long time. The small town has a lobster cooperative, a few streets with modest homes, and a lighthouse at the very end of the peninsula.

Cuzan Guest House ★ *Finds* This place has a rustic charm perfectly in character with its location at the end of the road, plus the great benefits of hot water, 24-hour solar electricity, comfortable beds, and private bathrooms. You have a choice of Maya-style stucco buildings with thatched roofs, concrete floors, and a combination of twin and king-size beds with mosquito netting, or raised wooden cabins with thatched roofs and little porches that overlook the water. These have two double beds each. The hotel's restaurant, a large *palapa* with a sand floor, serves three meals a day. Full breakfast and lunch run about $5 each, and dinner costs $12 to $15. The menu sometimes includes lobster in season (July–Apr). The food is good, and, of course, the seafood is fresh. Payment for meals must be in cash or traveler's checks.

Co-owner Sonja Lilvik, a Californian, offers fly-fishing trips for bone, permit, snook, and tarpon to the nearby saltwater flats and lagoons of Ascension Bay. One-week packages (priced per person, double occupancy) include lodging, three meals a day, a boat, and a guide. She also offers a fascinating 3-hour boat tour of the coastline that includes snorkeling, slipping in and out of mangrove-filled canals for birding, and skirting the edge of an island rookery loaded with frigate birds. November to March is frigate mating season, when the male shows off his big, billowy red breast pouch to impress potential mates. You can also go kayaking along the coast or relax in a hammock on the beach.

Punta Allen. (Reservations: Apdo. Postal 24, 77200 Felipe Carrillo Puerto, Q. Roo.) ✆ **983/834-0358.** Fax 983/834-0292. www.flyfishmx.com. 12 units. High season $40–$80 double. Low-season discounts available. All-inclusive fly-fishing packages $1,999 per week. No credit cards. **Amenities:** Restaurant; tours and activities desk. *In room:* No phone.

5

A Glimpse of the Maya: Nearby Ruins

As tempting as Cancún may be, the region surrounding the popular beach resort is even richer in natural and cultural pleasures. Those who bemoan the rather Americanized ways of Cancún will find that the Yucatán offers both authentic experiences and a relaxed charm. With a little exploring, you'll find a variety of things to do. This chapter covers the best-known Maya ruins of the Yucatán peninsula, including the seaside ruins of **Tulum,** the jungle complex at **Cobá,** and the supremely restored site at **Chichén Itzá.** These treasures are at once close to the easy air access of Cancún, yet miles away in mood and manner.

EXPLORING THE YUCATAN'S MAYA HEARTLAND

The best way to see the Yucatán is by car. The terrain is flat, there is little traffic, and the main highways are in good shape. If you do drive around the area, you will add one Spanish word to your vocabulary, which through much repetition will stick with you: *topes* (*toh-*pehs), or "speed bumps." *Topes* come in varying shapes and sizes and with varying degrees of warning. Don't let them catch you by surprise. Off the beaten path, the roads are narrow and rough, but hey—we're talking rental cars. Rentals are, in fact, a little pricey compared with those in the U.S. (due perhaps to wear and tear?), but some promotional deals are available, especially in the low season. For more on renting a car, see "Getting Around: By Car" in chapter 1.

Plenty of buses ply the roads between the major towns and ruins. And plenty of tour buses circulate, too. But buses to the smaller towns and ruins and the haciendas are infrequent or nonexistent. One bus company, Autobuses del Oriente (ADO), controls most of the first-class bus service and does a good job with the major destinations. Second-class buses go to some out-of-the-way places, but they can be slow, stop a lot, and aren't air-conditioned. I will take them when I'm going only a short distance, say around 25km

Tips What You Need to Know When Traveling in the Yucatán

The Yucatán is ***tierra caliente*** (the hotlands). Don't travel in this region without a hat, sunblock, mosquito repellent, and water. The coolest weather is from November to February; the hottest is from April to June. From July to October, thundershowers moderate temperatures. More tourists come to the interior during the winter months, but not to the same extent as on the Caribbean coast. The high-season/low-season distinction is less pronounced here.

(40 miles). If you don't want to rent a car, a few tour operators take small groups to more remote attractions such as ruins, *cenotes,* and villages.

1 Tulum ★

130km (80 miles) SW of Cancún

The walled Maya city of Tulum is a large post-Classic site overlooking the Caribbean in dramatic fashion. Tour companies and public buses make the trip regularly from Cancún and Playa del Carmen; get there early to avoid the crowds. Tulum also has wonderful, sandy beaches and no large resort hotels. It's a perfect spot for those who like to splash around in the water and lie on the beach away from the resort scene. The town has a dozen restaurants, five pharmacies, three cybercafes, a bank, two cash machines, and several stores.

ESSENTIALS

GETTING THERE **By Car** Drive south from Cancún on Highway 307; the ruins are 130km (81 miles) southwest of Cancún.

ORIENTATION Highway 307 passes the entrance to the ruins (on your left) before running through town. After the entrance to the ruins but before entering the town you'll come to a highway intersection with a traffic light. The light wasn't functioning the last time I was there. To the right is the highway leading to the ruins of Cobá (see "Cobá Ruins," later in this chapter); to the left is the Tulum hotel zone, which begins about 2km (1½ miles) away. The road sign reads BOCA PAILA, which is a place halfway down the **Punta Allen Peninsula** (see chapter 4). This road eventually goes all the way to the tip of the peninsula and the town of Punta Allen.

Tulum Ruins

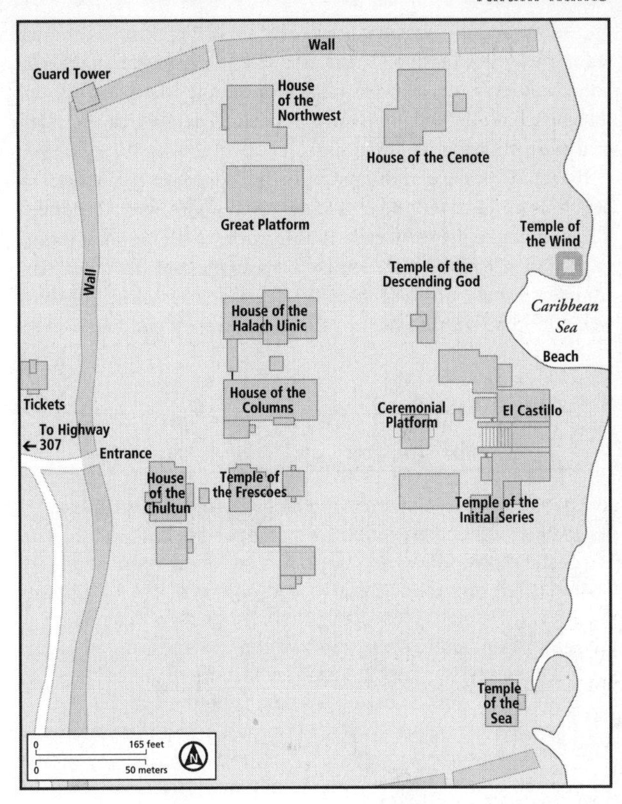

EXPLORING THE SITE

Thirteen kilometers (8 miles) south of Xel-Ha (see chapter 4) are the ruins of Tulum, a Maya fortress-city overlooking the Caribbean. The ruins are open to visitors daily from 7am to 5pm in the winter, 8am to 6pm in the summer. It's always best to go early, before the crowds start showing up (around 9:30am). The entrance to the ruins is about a 5-minute walk from the archaeological site. There are artisans' stands, a bookstore, a museum, a restaurant, several large bathrooms, and a ticket booth. Admission fee to the ruins is $4. If you want to ride the shuttle from the visitor center to the ruins, it's another $1.50. Parking is $3. A video camera permit costs $4. Licensed guides have a stand next to the path to the ruins and charge $20 for a 45-minute tour in English, French, or Spanish for up to four persons. In some ways, they are like performers and will tailor their presentation to the responses they receive from you. Some will try to draw connections between the Maya and Western theology. But they will point out architectural details that you might otherwise miss.

By A.D. 900, the end of the Classic period, Maya civilization had begun its decline, and the large cities to the south were abandoned. Tulum is one of the small city-states that rose to fill the void. It came to prominence in the 13th century as a seaport, controlling maritime commerce along this section of the coast, and remained inhabited well after the arrival of the Spanish. The primary god here was the

Fun Fact Tulum: A Friendly Difference of Opinion

Two of us cover the entirety of Mexico for Frommer's, and almost without exception we agree on the country's top destinations. However, we have an ongoing dialogue regarding the relative merits and beauty of the ruins at Tulum. Herewith we present our respective cases, and leave it for you to decide with whom you agree.

Lynne says: Ancient Tulum is my favorite of all the ruins, poised as it is on a rocky hill overlooking the transparent, turquoise Caribbean. It's not the largest or most important of the Maya ruins in this area, but it's the only one by the sea, which makes it the most visually impressive. Intriguing carvings and reliefs decorate the well-preserved structures, which date from the 12th to 16th centuries A.D., in the post-Classic period.

David says: Aside from the spectacular setting, Tulum is not as impressive a city as Chichén Itzá, Uxmal, or Ek Balam. The stonework is cruder than that at these other sites, as if construction of the platforms and temples had been hurried. The city's builders were concerned foremost with security and defense. They chose the most rugged section on this coast and then built stout walls on the other three sides. This must have absorbed a tremendous amount of energy that might otherwise have been used to build the large ceremonial centers and more varied architecture we see elsewhere in the Yucatán.

diving god, depicted on several buildings as an upside-down figure above doorways. Seen at the Palace at Sayil and Cobá, this curious, almost comical figure is also known as the bee god.

The most imposing building in Tulum is a large stone structure above the cliff called the **Castillo (castle).** Actually a temple as well as a fortress, it was once covered with stucco and painted. In front of the Castillo are several unrestored palacelike buildings partially covered with stucco. On the **beach** below, where the Maya once came ashore, tourists swim and sunbathe, combining a visit to the ruins with a dip in the Caribbean.

The **Temple of the Frescoes,** directly in front of the Castillo, contains interesting 13th-century wall paintings, though entrance is no longer permitted. Distinctly Maya, they represent the rain god Chaac and Ixchel, the goddess of weaving, women, the moon, and medicine. On the cornice of this temple is a relief of the head of the rain god. If you pause a slight distance from the building, you'll see the eyes, nose, mouth, and chin. Notice the remains of the red-painted stucco—at one time all the buildings at Tulum were painted bright red.

Much of what we know of Tulum at the time of the Spanish Conquest comes from the writings of Diego de Landa, third bishop of the Yucatán. He wrote that Tulum was a small city inhabited by about 600 people who lived in platform dwellings along a street and who supervised the trade traffic from Honduras to the Yucatán. Though it was a walled city, most of the inhabitants probably lived outside the walls, leaving the interior for the residences of governors and priests and ceremonial structures. Tulum survived about 70 years after the Conquest, when it was finally abandoned. Because of the great number of visitors this site receives, it is no longer possible to climb all of the ruins. In many cases, visitors are asked to remain behind roped-off areas to view them.

WHERE TO STAY IN & AROUND TULUM

This stretch of coast has great beaches. The seven or eight hotels in town are cheaper than all but the most basic of beach accommodations, but they aren't as much fun. They offer no-frills lodging for $20 to $50 a night. All the beach hotels must generate their own electricity, and this raises the price of lodging. Most of them are simple affairs without a lot of luxuries. Turn east at the highway intersection. Three kilometers (2 miles) ahead, you come to a T junction. North are most of the cheap cabañas. Over the years, I've heard from several sources about cases of theft at a few of these establishments.

To the south are most of the *palapa* hotels, including some moderately priced lodging. The pavement quickly turns into sand, and on both sides of the road you start seeing cabañas. You can try your luck at one of many places. The rates listed below don't include the week of Christmas and New Year, when prices go above regular high season rates.

EXPENSIVE

Hotel Nueva Vida ★ I like this place because it's so different, with few rooms, much space, and an ecological orientation. It has 150m (500 ft.) of beautiful beachfront, but the cabañas are built behind the beach, in the jungle, which has been preserved as much as possible. Most of the rooms are in freestanding thatched cabañas 4m (12 ft.) off the ground. Each is midsize with a private bathroom, a double and a twin bed with mosquito netting, and a ceiling fan (solar cells and wind generators provide energy 24 hr. a day; there are no electrical outlets in the units). There are also some junior suites housed in a two-story building, which are larger and come with a few more amenities, also there are some two-bedroom units, which go for a bit more than the junior suites. The owners are from South America and operate a family-style restaurant.

Carretera Punta Allen Km 8.5, 77780 Tulum, Q. Roo. ✆ **984/877-8512.** Fax 984/871-2092. www.tulumnv.com. 9 units. High season $132 double, $181 suite; low season $83 double, $122 suite. Rates include continental breakfast. MC, V. **Amenities:** Restaurant; tour information; limited room service; massage; laundry service; nonsmoking rooms. *In room:* No phone.

Restaurant y Cabañas Ana y José ★★ This comfortable hotel sits on a great beach with a good beach restaurant. The rock-walled cabañas in front (called "oceanfront"), closest to the water, are a little larger than the others and come with two double beds. I also like the attractive second-floor oceanview rooms, which have tall *palapa* roofs. The garden-view rooms are much like the others but don't face the sea. Newer construction has crowded them in back, making them much less desirable. There is 24-hour electricity for lights and ceiling fans. Sometimes you can book a package deal that includes hotel and a rental car waiting for you at the Cancún airport. Ana y José is 6.5km (4 miles) south of the Tulum ruins.

Carretera Punta Allen Km 7 (Apdo. Postal 15), 77780 Tulum, Q. Roo. ✆ **998/887-5470** in Cancún. Fax 998/887-5469. www.anayjose.com. 21 units. High season $206–$276 double, $296 suite; low season $130–$200 double, $220 suite. AE, MC, V. Free parking. **Amenities:** Restaurant; small pool; spa; tour info; car rental. *In room:* No phone.

MODERATE

Cabañas Tulum Next to Ana y José is a row of cinderblock facing the same beautiful ocean and beach. These accommodations are basic. Rooms are simple, not unattractive, though poorly lit. The bathrooms are ample. All rooms have two double beds (most with new mattresses), screens on the windows, a table, one electric light, and a porch facing the beach. Electricity is available from 7 to 11am and 6 to 11pm.

Carretera Punta Allen Km 7 (Apdo. Postal 63), 77780 Tulum, Q. Roo. ✆ **984/879-7395.** Fax 984/871-2092. www.hotelstulum.com. 32 units. $70–$100 double. No credit cards. **Amenities:** Restaurant; game room.

Retiro Maya *Retiro* is Spanish for retreat, and the word is used aptly here. I suspect that the English-speaking owner, Lu Montiel, was looking for something that would be the exact opposite of her native Mexico City. This place is it—supremely quiet and lit only by candles. The 12 attractive Maya-style cottages are arranged for privacy on 50m (165 ft.) of immaculate beachfront. Each has a king-size bed draped in mosquito netting. There is no electricity, just candles. There is no floor, only swept sand. The units share a common bathroom area. A restaurant has reasonable prices and good food.

Carretera Punta Allen Km 6.5 (Apdo. Postal 166), 77780 Tulum, Q. Roo. ✆ **998/101-1154.** www.retiromaya.com. 12 units. $90–$115 double with shared bathroom. No credit cards. No children. **Amenities:** Restaurant. *In room:* No phone.

Zamas ★★ The owners of these cabañas, a couple from San Francisco, have made their rustic getaway most enjoyable by concentrating on the essentials: comfort, privacy, and good food. The cabañas are simple, attractive, well situated for catching the breeze, and not too close together. Most rooms are in individual structures; the suites and oversize rooms are in modest two-story buildings. For the money, I like the six individual garden *palapas,* which are attractive and comfortable, with either two double beds or a double and a twin. Two small beachfront cabañas with one double bed go for a little less. The most expensive rooms are the upstairs oceanview units, which enjoy a large terrace and lots of sea breezes. I like these especially. They come with a king-size and a queen-size bed or a double and a queen-size bed. The restaurant serves fresh seafood—I've seen the owner actually flag down passing fishermen to buy their catch. A white-sand beach stretches between large rocky areas.

Carretera Punta Allen Km 5, 77780 Tulum, Q. Roo. ✆ **415/387-9806** in the U.S. www.zamas.com. 20 units. High season $90–$130 beachfront double, $100 garden double, $120–$155 oceanview double; low season $65–$95 beachfront double, $65 garden double, $85–$110 oceanview double. No credit cards. **Amenities:** Restaurant.

WHERE TO DINE

There are several restaurants in the town of Tulum. They are reasonably priced and do an okay job. On the main street are **Charlie's** (**© 984/871-2136**), my favorite for Mexican food, and **Don Cafeto's** (**© 984/871-2207**). A good Italian-owned Italian restaurant, **Il Giardino di Toni e Simone** (**© 984/804-1316**; closed Wed), is 1 block off the highway—you'll see a large building-supply store called ROCA. It's on the opposite side of the road, 1 block away. Also in town are a couple of roadside places that grill chicken and serve it with rice and beans. Out on the coast, you can eat at **Zamas** or at **Ana y José** (see above).

2 Cobá Ruins

168km (105 miles) SW of Cancún

Older than most of Chichén Itzá and much larger than Tulum, Cobá was the dominant city of the eastern Yucatán before A.D. 1000. The site is large and spread out, with thick forest growing between the temple groups. Rising high above the forest canopy are tall, steep classic Maya pyramids. Of the major sites, this one is the least reconstructed and so disappoints those who expect another Chichén Itzá. Appreciating it requires a greater exercise of the imagination. Bordering the ruins are two lakes, an uncommon feature in the Yucatán, where surface water is rare.

ESSENTIALS

GETTING THERE & DEPARTING **By Car** The road to Cobá begins in Tulum, across Highway 307 from the turnoff to the Punta Allen Peninsula. Turn right when you see signs for Cobá, and continue on that road for 65km (40 miles). Watch out for both *topes* (speed bumps) and potholes. Enter the village, proceed straight until you see the lake, then turn left. The entrance to the ruins is a short distance down the road past some small restaurants. There's a large parking area.

By Bus Several buses a day leave Tulum and Playa del Carmen for Cobá. Several companies offer bus tours.

EXPLORING THE RUINS

The Maya built many intriguing cities in the Yucatán, but few grander than Cobá ("water stirred by wind"). Much of the 67-sq.-km

Cobá Ruins

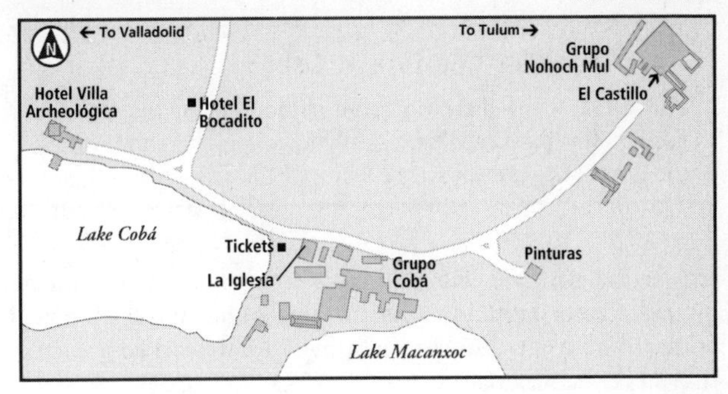

(26-sq.-mile) site remains unexcavated. A 100km (60-mile) *sacbé* (a pre-Hispanic raised road or causeway) through the jungle linked Cobá to Yaxuná, once a large, important Maya center 50km (30 miles) south of Chichén Itzá. It's the Maya's longest known *sacbé,* and at least 50 shorter ones lead from here. An important city-state, Cobá flourished from A.D. 632 (the oldest carved date found here) until after the rise of Chichén Itzá, around 800. Then Cobá slowly faded in importance and population until it was finally abandoned. Scholars believe Cobá was an important trade link between the Yucatán Caribbean coast and inland cities.

Once at the site, keep your bearings—you can get turned around in the maze of dirt roads in the jungle. And bring bug spray. As spread out as this city is, renting a bike (which you can do at the entrance for $2.50) is a good option. Branching off from every labeled path, you'll notice unofficial narrow paths into the jungle, used by locals as shortcuts through the ruins. These are good for birding, but be careful to remember the way back.

The **Grupo Cobá** boasts an impressive pyramid, **La Iglesia (The Church),** which you'll find if you take the path bearing right after the entrance. As you approach, notice the unexcavated mounds on the left. Though the urge to climb the temple is great, the view is better from El Castillo in the Nohoch Mul group farther back.

From here, return to the main path and turn right. You'll pass a sign pointing right to the ruined ***juego de pelota*** **(ball court),** but the path is obscure.

Continuing straight ahead on this path for 5 to 10 minutes, you'll come to a fork in the road. To the left and right you'll notice jungle-covered, unexcavated pyramids, and at one point, you'll see a raised portion crossing the pathway—this is the visible remains of the

Tips For Your Comfort at Cobá

Visit Cobá in the morning or after the heat of the day has passed. Mosquito repellent, drinking water, and comfortable shoes are imperative.

sacbé to Yaxuná. Throughout the area, intricately carved steles stand by pathways or lie forlornly in the jungle underbrush. Although protected by crude thatched roofs, most are weatherworn enough that they're indiscernible.

The left fork leads to the **Nohoch Mul Group,** which contains **El Castillo.** With the exception of Structure 2 in Calakmul, this is the tallest pyramid in the Yucatán (rising even higher than the great El Castillo at Chichén Itzá and the Pyramid of the Magician at Uxmal). So far, visitors are still permitted to climb to the top. From this magnificent lofty perch, you can see unexcavated jungle-covered pyramidal structures poking up through the forest all around.

The right fork (more or less straight on) goes to the **Conjunto Las Pinturas.** Here, the main attraction is the **Pyramid of the Painted Lintel,** a small structure with traces of its original bright colors above the door. You can climb up to get a close look. Though maps of Cobá show ruins around two lakes, there are really only two excavated groups.

Admission is $4, free for children under age 12. Parking is $1. A video camera permit costs $4. The site is open daily from 8am to 5pm, sometimes longer.

WHERE TO STAY & DINE

El Bocadito El Bocadito, on the right as you enter town (next to the hotel's restaurant of the same name), offers rooms arranged in two rows facing an open patio. They're simple, with tile floors, two double beds, no bedspreads, a ceiling fan, and a washbasin separate from the toilet and cold-water shower cubicle. The open-air restaurant offers good meals at reasonable prices, served by a friendly, efficient staff.

Calle Principal, Cobá, Q. Roo. (Reservations: Apdo. Postal 56, 97780 Valladolid, Yuc.) No phone. 8 units. $18–$25 double. No credit cards. Free unguarded parking. **Amenities:** Restaurant. *In room:* No phone.

Villas Arqueológicas Cobá This lovely lakeside hotel is a 5-minute walk from the ruins. It is laid out like its Club Med counterparts in Chichén Itzá and Uxmal. The beautiful grounds hold a pool and tennis court. The restaurant is top-notch, though expensive, and the rooms are stylish and modern, but small. Beds occupy niches that surround the mattress on three sides and can be somewhat uncomfortable for those taller than about 2m (6 ft.). The hotel also has a library on Mesoamerican archaeology (with books in French, English, and Spanish). Make reservations—this hotel fills with touring groups.

Cobá, Q. Roo. ✆ **800/258-2633** in the U.S., or 55/5203-3086 in Mexico City. 41 units. $105 double. Rates include continental breakfast. Half-board (breakfast plus lunch or dinner) $15 per person; full board (3 meals) $30 per person. AE, MC, V. Free guarded parking. Drive through town and turn right at lake; hotel is straight ahead on the right. **Amenities:** Restaurant; bar; midsize pool. *In room:* No phone.

3 The Ruins of Chichén Itzá ★★★

179km (112 miles) W of Cancún; 120km (75 miles) E of Mérida

The fabled pyramids and temples of Chichén Itzá (no, it doesn't rhyme with "chicken pizza"; the accents are on the last syllables: Chee-*chen* Eet-*zah*) are the Yucatán's best-known ancient monuments. The ruins are plenty hyped, but Chichén is truly worth seeing. Walking among these stone platforms, pyramids, and ball courts gives you an appreciation for this ancient civilization that books cannot convey. The city is built on a scale that evokes a sense of wonder: To fill the plazas during one of the mass rituals that occurred here a millennium ago would have required an enormous number of celebrants. Even today, with the mass flow of tourists through these plazas, the ruins feel empty.

When visiting this old city, remember that much of what is said about the Maya (especially by tour guides, who speak in tones of utter certainty) is merely educated guessing—or just plain guessing. Itzáes established this post-Classic Maya city perhaps sometime during the 9th century A.D. Linda Schele and David Freidel, in *A Forest of Kings* (Morrow, 1990), have cast doubt on the legend of its founding. It says that the Toltec, led by Kukulkán (Quetzalcoatl), came here from the Toltec capital of Tula, in north-central Mexico. Along with Putún Maya coastal traders, they built a magnificent metropolis that combined the Maya Puuc style with Toltec motifs (the feathered serpent, warriors, eagles, and jaguars). Not so, say Schele and Freidel. According to them, readings of Chichén's bas-reliefs and hieroglyphs fail to support that legend and, instead, show that Chichén Itzá was a continuous Maya site influenced by association with the Toltec but not by an invasion. Not all scholars embrace this thinking, so the idea of a Toltec invasion still holds sway.

Though it's possible to make a round-trip from Mérida to Chichén Itzá in a day, it will be a long, tiring, very rushed day. Try to spend at least a night at Chichén Itzá (you will already have paid for the sound-and-light show) or the nearby town of Valladolid. Then you can see the ruins early the next morning when it is cool and before the tour buses arrive.

ESSENTIALS

GETTING THERE & DEPARTING **By Plane** Travel agents in the United States and Cancún can arrange day trips from Cancún.

By Car Chichén Itzá is on old Highway 180 between Mérida and Cancún. The fastest way to get there from either city is to take the *autopista* (or *cuota*). The toll is $8 from Mérida, $20 from Cancún. Once you have exited the *autopista,* you will turn onto the road leading to the village of Pisté. After you enter the village, you'll come to Highway 180, where you turn left. Signs point the way. Chichén is 1½ hours from Mérida and 2½ hours from Cancún.

By Bus From Mérida, there are three first-class ADO buses per day, and a couple that go to Valladolid stop here. Also, there are several second-class buses per day. If you want to take a day trip from Mérida, go with a tour company. From Cancún, there are any number of tourist buses, and regular first-class buses leave for Chichén every hour.

Tips The Best Websites for Chichén Itzá & the Maya Interior

- **National Geographic: www.nationalgeographic.com** A fascinating collection of articles from *National Geographic* and other sources.
- **Yucatán Travel Guide: www.mayayucatan.com** Yucatán's newly formed Ministry of Tourism maintains this site. It has an update section and good general info on different destinations in the state.
- **Mexico's Yucatán Directory: www.mexonline.com/yucatan.htm** A nice roundup of vacation rentals, tour operators, and information on the Maya sites. For more information on Mexico's indigenous history, see the links on the pre-Columbian page (www.mexonline.com/precolum.htm).

Chichén Itzá Ruins

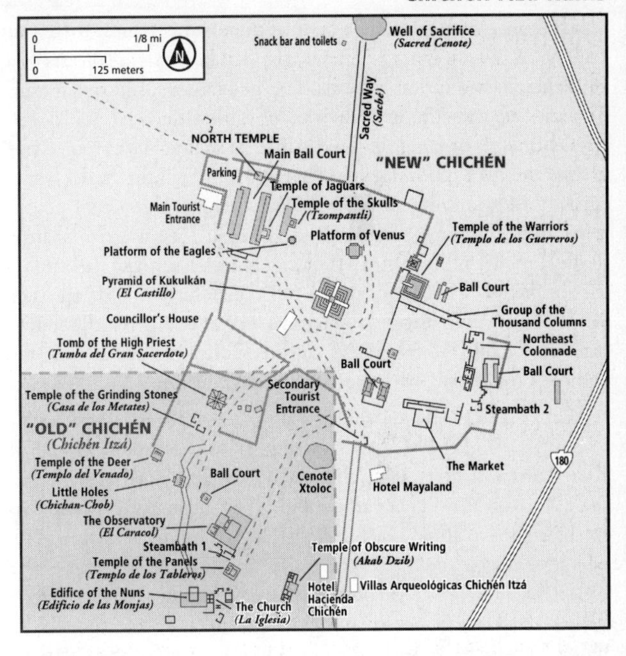

ORIENTATION The village of **Pisté,** where most hotels and restaurants are located, is about 2.5km (1½ miles) from the ruins of Chichén Itzá. Public buses from Mérida, Cancún, Valladolid, and elsewhere discharge passengers here. A few hotels are at the edge of the ruins, and one, the Hotel Dolores Alba (see "Where to Stay," later in this chapter), is out of town about 2.5km (1½ miles) from the ruins on the road to Valladolid.

EXPLORING THE RUINS

The site occupies 6.5 sq. km (4 sq. miles), and it takes most of a day to see all the ruins, which are open daily from 8am to 5pm. Service areas are open from 8am to 10pm. Admission is $10, free for children under age 12. A video camera permit costs $4. Parking is extra. *You can use your ticket to reenter on the same day, but you'll have to pay again for an additional day.* The cost of admission includes the **sound-and-light show,** which is worth seeing. The show, held at 7 or 8pm depending on the season, is in Spanish, but headsets are available for rent ($4.50) in several languages.

The large, modern visitor center, at the main entrance where you pay the admission charge, is beside the parking lot and consists of a museum, an auditorium, a restaurant, a bookstore, and bathrooms. You can see the site on your own or with a licensed guide who speaks English or Spanish. Guides usually wait at the entrance and charge around $40 for one to six people. Although the guides frown on it, there's nothing wrong with approaching a group of people who speak the same language and asking if they want to share a guide. Be wary of the history-spouting guides—some of their information is just plain out-of-date—but the architectural details they point out are enlightening. Chichén Itzá has two parts: the northern (new) zone, which shows distinct Toltec influence, and the southern (old) zone, with mostly Puuc architecture.

EL CASTILLO As you enter from the tourist center, the magnificent 25m (75-ft.) El Castillo pyramid (also called the Pyramid of Kukulkán) will be straight ahead across a large open area. It was built with the Maya calendar in mind. The four stairways leading up to the central platform each have 91 steps, making a total of 364, which when you add the central platform equals the 365 days of the solar year. On either side of each stairway are nine terraces, which makes 18 on each face of the pyramid, equaling the number of months in the Maya solar calendar. On the facing of these terraces are 52 panels (we don't know how they were decorated), which represent the 52-year cycle when both the solar and religious calendars would become realigned. The pyramid's alignment is such that on the **spring** or **fall equinox** (Mar 21 or Sept 21) a curious event occurs. The setting sun casts the shadow of the terraces onto the ramp of the northern stairway. A diamond pattern is formed, suggestive of the geometric designs on some snakes. Slowly it descends into the earth. The effect is more conceptual than visual, and to view it requires being with a large crowd. It's much better to see the ruins on other days when it's less crowded.

El Castillo was built over an earlier structure. A narrow stairway at the western edge of the north staircase leads inside that structure, where there is a sacrificial altar-throne—a red jaguar encrusted with jade. The stairway is open from 11am to 3pm and is cramped, usually crowded, humid, and uncomfortable. A visit early in the day is best. Photos of the jaguar figure are not allowed.

JUEGO DE PELOTA (MAIN BALL COURT) Northwest of El Castillo is Chichén's main ball court, the largest and best preserved anywhere, and only one of nine ball courts built in this city. Carved on both walls of the ball court are scenes showing Maya figures dressed as ball players and decked out in heavy protective padding. The carved scene also shows a headless player kneeling with blood shooting from his neck; another player holding the head looks on.

Players on two teams tried to knock a hard rubber ball through one of the two stone rings placed high on either wall, using only their elbows, knees, and hips (no hands). According to legend, the losing players paid for defeat with their lives. However, some experts say the victors were the only appropriate sacrifices for the gods. One can only guess what the incentive for winning might be in that case. Either way, the game must have been riveting, heightened by the wonderful acoustics of the ball court.

THE NORTH TEMPLE Temples are at both ends of the ball court. The North Temple has sculptured pillars and more sculptures inside, as well as badly ruined murals. The acoustics of the ball court are so good that from the North Temple, a person speaking can be heard clearly at the opposite end, about 135m (450 ft.) away.

TEMPLE OF JAGUARS Near the southeastern corner of the main ball court is a small temple with serpent columns and carved panels showing warriors and jaguars. Up the steps and inside the temple, a mural was found that chronicles a battle in a Maya village.

TZOMPANTLI (TEMPLE OF THE SKULLS) To the right of the ball court is the Temple of the Skulls, an obvious borrowing from the post-Classic cities of central Mexico. Notice the rows of skulls carved into the stone platform. When a sacrificial victim's head was cut off, it was impaled on a pole and displayed in a tidy row with others. Also carved into the stone are pictures of eagles tearing hearts from human victims. The word *Tzompantli* is not Mayan but comes from central Mexico. Reconstruction using scattered fragments may add a level to this platform and change the look of this structure by the time you visit.

PLATFORM OF THE EAGLES Next to the Tzompantli, this small platform has reliefs showing eagles and jaguars clutching human hearts in their talons and claws, as well as a human head emerging from the mouth of a serpent.

PLATFORM OF VENUS East of the Tzompantli and north of El Castillo, near the road to the Sacred *Cenote,* is the Platform of Venus. In Maya and Toltec lore, a feathered monster or a feathered serpent with a human head in its mouth represented Venus. This is also called the tomb of Chaac-Mool because a Chaac-Mool figure was discovered "buried" within the structure.

SACRED *CENOTE* Follow the dirt road (actually an ancient *sacbé,* or causeway) that heads north from the Platform of Venus; after 5 minutes you'll come to the great natural well that may have given Chichén Itzá (the Well of the Itzáes) its name. This well was used for ceremonial purposes, not for drinking water—according to legend, sacrificial victims were drowned in this pool to honor the rain god Chaac. Anatomical research done early in the 20th century by Ernest A. Hooten showed that bones of both children and adults were found in the well. Judging from Hooten's evidence, they may have been outcasts or diseased or feeble-minded persons.

Edward Thompson, who was the American consul in Mérida and a Harvard professor, purchased the ruins of Chichén early in the 20th century and explored the *cenote* with dredges and divers. His explorations exposed a fortune in gold and jade. Most of the riches wound up in Harvard's Peabody Museum of Archaeology and Ethnology—a matter that continues to disconcert Mexican classicists today. Excavations in the 1960s unearthed more treasure, and studies of the recovered objects detail offerings from throughout the Yucatán and even farther away.

TEMPLO DE LOS GUERREROS (TEMPLE OF THE WARRIORS) Due east of El Castillo is one of the most impressive structures at Chichén: the Temple of the Warriors, named for the carvings of warriors marching along its walls. It's also called the Group of the Thousand Columns for the rows of broken pillars that flank it. During the recent restoration, hundreds more of the columns were rescued from the rubble and put in place, setting off the temple more magnificently than ever. A figure of Chaac-Mool sits at the top of the temple, surrounded by impressive columns carved in relief to look like enormous feathered serpents. South of the temple was a square building that archaeologists called ***El Mercado* (The Market);** a colonnade surrounds its central court. Beyond the temple and the market in the jungle are mounds of rubble, parts of which are being reconstructed.

The main Mérida-Cancún highway once ran straight through the ruins of Chichén, and though it has been diverted, you can still see the great swath it cut. South and west of the old highway's path are more impressive ruined buildings.

TUMBA DEL GRAN SACERDOTE (TOMB OF THE HIGH PRIEST) Past the refreshment stand to the right of the path is the Tomb of the High Priest, which stood atop a natural limestone cave in which skeletons and offerings were found, giving the temple its name.

CASA DE LOS METATES (TEMPLE OF THE GRINDING STONES) This building, the next one on your right, is named after the concave corn-grinding stones the Maya used.

TEMPLO DEL VENADO (TEMPLE OF THE DEER) Past Casa de los Metates is this fairly tall though ruined building. The relief of a stag that gave the temple its name is long gone.

CHICHAN-CHOB (LITTLE HOLES) This next temple has a roof comb with little holes, three masks of the rain god Chaac, three rooms, and a good view of the surrounding structures. It's one of the oldest buildings at Chichén, built in the Puuc style during the late Classic period.

EL CARACOL (OBSERVATORY) Construction of the Observatory, a complex building with a circular tower, was carried out over centuries; the additions and modifications reflected the Maya's careful observation of celestial movements and their need for increasingly exact measurements. Through slits in the tower's walls, astronomers could observe the cardinal directions and the approach of the all-important spring and autumn equinoxes, as well as the summer solstice. The temple's name, which means "snail," comes from a spiral staircase within the structure.

On the east side of El Caracol, a path leads north into the bush to the **Cenote Xtoloc,** a natural limestone well that provided the city's daily water supply. If you see any lizards sunning there, they may well be *xtoloc,* the species for which this *cenote* is named.

TEMPLO DE LOS TABLEROS (TEMPLE OF PANELS) Just south of El Caracol are the ruins of *temazcalli* (a steam bath) and the Temple of Panels, named for the carved panels on top. This temple was once covered by a much larger structure, only traces of which remain.

EDIFICIO DE LAS MONJAS (EDIFICE OF THE NUNS) If you've visited the Puuc sites of Kabah, Sayil, Labná, or Xlapak, the enormous nunnery here will remind you of the palaces at those sites. Built in the Late Classic period, the new edifice was constructed over an older one. Suspecting that this was so, Le Plongeon, an archaeologist working early in the 20th century, put dynamite between the two and blew away part of the exterior, revealing the older structures within. You can still see the results of Le Plongeon's indelicate exploratory methods.

On the east side of the Edifice of the Nuns is **Anexo Este (annex)** constructed in highly ornate Chenes style with Chaac masks and serpents.

LA IGLESIA (THE CHURCH) Next to the annex is one of the oldest buildings at Chichén, the Church. Masks of Chaac decorate two upper stories. Look closely, and you'll see other pagan symbols among the crowd of Chaacs: an armadillo, a crab, a snail, and a tortoise. These represent the Maya gods, called *bacah,* whose job it was to hold up the sky.

AKAB DZIB (TEMPLE OF OBSCURE WRITING) This temple lies east of the Edifice of the Nuns. Above a door in one of the rooms are some Maya glyphs, which gave the temple its name because the writings have yet to be deciphered. In other rooms, traces of red handprints are still visible. Reconstructed and expanded over the centuries, Akab Dzib may be the oldest building at Chichén.

CHICHEN VIEJO (OLD CHICHEN) For a look at more of Chichén's oldest buildings, constructed well before the time of Toltec influence, follow signs from the Edifice of the Nuns southwest into the bush to Old Chichén, about 1km (½ mile) away. Be prepared for this trek with long trousers, insect repellent, and a local guide. The attractions here are the **Templo de los Inscripciones Iniciales (Temple of the First Inscriptions),** with the oldest inscriptions discovered at Chichén, and the restored **Templo de los Dinteles (Temple of the Lintels),** a fine Puuc building.

WHERE TO STAY

The expensive hotels in Chichén all occupy beautiful grounds, are close to the ruins, and serve good food. All have toll-free reservations numbers. Some of these hotels do a lot of business with tour operators—they can be empty one day and full the next. The inexpensive hotels are in the village of Pisté, 2.5km (1½ miles) away. There is little to do in Pisté at night. Another option is to go on to the colonial town of Valladolid, 30 minutes away, but you'll want reservations because a lot of tour-bus companies use the hotels there.

EXPENSIVE

Hacienda Chichén ★★ This is the smallest and most private of the hotels at the ruins. It is also the quietest. This former hacienda served as the headquarters for the Carnegie Institute's excavations in

1923. Several bungalows were built to house the staff; these have been modernized and are now the guest rooms. Each is simply and comfortably furnished (with a dehumidifier and ceiling fan in addition to air-conditioning) and is a short distance from the others. Each bungalow has a private porch from which you can enjoy the beautiful grounds. Standard rooms come with two twin or two double beds. Suites are bigger and have larger bathrooms and double or queen-size beds. The main building belonged to the hacienda; it houses the terrace restaurant, with dining outside by the pool or inside.

Zona Arqueológica, 97751 Chichén Itzá, Yuc. ✆/fax **985/851-0045.** www.yucatanadventure.com.mx. (Reservations: Casa del Balam, Calle 60 no. 488, 97000 Mérida, Yuc. ✆ **800/624-8451** in the U.S., or 999/924-2150. Fax 999/924-5011.) 28 units. $150 double; $165 suite. AE, DC, MC, V. Free guarded parking. **Amenities:** Restaurant; bar; large pool. *In room:* A/C, minibar, hair dryer.

Hotel Mayaland ★★ The main doorway frames El Caracol (the observatory) in a stunning view—that's how close this hotel is to the ruins. The long main building is three stories high. The rooms are large, with comfortable beds and large tiled bathrooms. Bungalows, scattered about the rest of the grounds, are built native style, with thatched roofs and stucco walls; they're a good deal larger than the rooms. The grounds are gorgeous, with huge trees and lush foliage—the hotel has had 75 years to get them in shape. The suites are on the top floor of the main building and come with terraces and two-person Jacuzzis. The "lodge section" consists of two groupings of larger bungalows in the back of the property surrounded by a lovely garden and pool area—they are separate from the main hotel and offer greater privacy and quiet.

Zona Arqueológica, 97751 Chichén Itzá, Yuc. ✆ **985/851-0127.** (Reservations: Mayaland Resorts, Robalo 30 SM3, 77500 Cancún, Q. Roo. ✆ **800/235-4079** in the U.S., or 998/887-0870. Fax 998/884-4510.) www.mayaland.com. 97 units. Nov $190 double, $240–$290 bungalow, $290–$350 suite, $268–$330 lodge section; Dec–Apr $148 double, $218–$245 bungalow, $245–$320 suite, $244–$295 lodge section; May–Oct $88 double, $144–$196 bungalow, $196–$235 suite, $144–$264 lodge section. Higher rates are for units with Jacuzzi. AE, MC, V. Free guarded parking. **Amenities:** 2 restaurants; bar; 3 pools; tour desk; room service until 10pm; babysitting; laundry service. *In room:* A/C, TV, minibar, coffeemaker.

Villas Arqueológicas Chichén Itzá ★ This hotel is built around a courtyard and a pool. Two massive royal poinciana trees tower above the grounds, and bougainvillea drapes the walls. This chain has similar hotels at Cobá and Uxmal, and is connected with Club Med. The rooms are modern and small but comfortable, unless you're 1.9m (6 ft., 2 in.) or taller—each bed is in a niche, with walls at the head and foot. Most rooms have one double bed and an oversize single bed. You can also book a half- or full-board plan.

Zona Arqueológica, 97751 Chichén Itzá, Yuc. ✆ **800/258-2633** in the U.S., or 985/851-0034 or 985/856-2830. 40 units. $90 double. Rates include continental breakfast. Half-board (breakfast plus lunch or dinner) $15 per person; full board (3 meals) $29 per person. AE, MC, V. Free parking. **Amenities:** Restaurant; bar; large pool; tennis court; tour desk. *In room:* A/C.

MODERATE

Hotel Dolores Alba ★ *Value* This place is of the motel variety, perfect if you come by car. It is a bargain for what you get: two pools (one really special), *palapas* and hammocks around the place, and large, comfortable rooms. The restaurant serves good meals at moderate prices. The hotel provides free transportation to the ruins and the Caves of Balankanché during visiting hours, though you will have to take a taxi back. The hotel is on the highway 2.5km (1½ miles) east of the ruins (toward Valladolid). You can make reservations here for the Dolores Alba in Mérida.

Carretera Mérida–Valladolid Km 122, Yuc. ✆ **985/858-1555.** (Reservations: Hotel Dolores Alba, Calle 63 no. 464, 97000 Mérida, Yuc. ✆ **999/928-5650.** Fax 999/928-3163.) www.doloresalba.com. 40 units. $50 double. No credit cards. Free parking. **Amenities:** Restaurant; bar; 2 pools; room service until midnight; laundry service. *In room:* A/C.

Pirámide Inn Less than 1.5km (1 mile) from the ruins, at the edge of Pisté, this hotel has simple rooms. Most hold two double beds, some three twins or one king-size. The bathrooms are nice, with counter space and tub/shower combinations. The air-conditioning is quiet and effective. Hot water comes on between 5 and 10am and 5 and 10pm. A well-kept pool and a *temazcal* (a native form of steam bath) occupy a small part of the landscaped grounds, which include the remains of a Maya wall. Try to get a room in the back—the hotel is right on the highway. There's a discount for those paying in cash.

Calle 15 no. 30, 97751 Pisté, Yuc. ✆ **985/851-0115.** Fax 985/851-0114. www.piramideinn.com. 44 units. $55 double. MC, V. **Amenities:** Restaurant; bar; midsize pool; steam room; room service. *In room:* A/C.

WHERE TO DINE

The restaurant in the visitor center at the ruins and the hotel restaurants in Pisté serve reasonably priced meals. Many places cater to large groups, which descend on them after 1pm.

Cafetería Ruinas INTERNATIONAL Though it has the monopoly on food at the ruins, this cafeteria does a good job with such basic meals as enchiladas, pizza, and baked chicken. It even offers some Yucatecan dishes. Eggs and burgers are cooked to order, and the coffee is good. You can also get fruit smoothies and vegetarian dishes.

In the Chichén Itzá visitor center. ✆ **985/851-0111.** Breakfast $5; sandwiches $6–$7; main courses $5–$10. AE, MC, V. Daily 9am–6pm.

Fiesta YUCATECAN/MEXICAN Though relatively expensive, the food here is dependable and good. You can dine inside or out, but make a point of going for supper or early lunch when the tour buses are gone. There is a full buffet, and the a la carte menu has many Yucatecan classics. Fiesta is on the west end of town.

Carretera Mérida–Valladolid, Pisté. ✆ **985/851-0038.** Main courses $4–$6; buffet (12:30–5pm) $8.50. No credit cards. Daily 7am–9pm.

Restaurant Bar "Poxil" YUCATECAN A *poxil* is a Maya fruit somewhat akin to a *guanábana.* Although this place doesn't serve them, what is on the simple menu is good, but not gourmet, and the price is right. You will find the Poxil near the west entrance to town on the south side of the street.

Calle 15 no. 52, Pisté. ✆ **985/851-0123.** Main courses $4–$5; breakfast $3. No credit cards. Daily 8am–9pm.

A SIDE TRIP TO THE GRUTA (CAVE) DE BALANKANCHE

The Gruta de Balankanché is 5.5km (3½ miles) from Chichén Itzá on the road to Valladolid and Cancún. Taxis will make the trip and wait. The entire excursion takes about a half-hour, but the walk inside is hot and humid. Of the cave tours in the Yucatán, this is the tamest, having good footing and requiring the least amount of walking and climbing. It includes a cheesy and uninformative recorded tour. The highlight is a round chamber with a central column that gives the impression of being a large tree. You come up the same way you go down. The cave became a hideaway during the War of the Castes. You can still see traces of carving and incense burning, as well as an underground stream that served as the sanctuary's water supply. Outside, take time to meander through the botanical gardens, where most of the plants and trees are labeled with their common and scientific names.

The caves are open daily. Admission is $5, free for children 6 to 12. Children under age 6 are not admitted. Use of a video camera costs $4 (free if you've already bought a video permit in Chichén the same day). Tours in English are at 11am and 1 and 3pm, and, in Spanish, at 9am, noon, and 2 and 4pm. Double-check these hours at the main entrance to the Chichén ruins.

Appendix: Useful Terms & Phrases

1 Basic Vocabulary

Most Mexicans are very patient with foreigners who try to speak their language; it helps a lot to know a few basic phrases. I've included simple phrases for expressing basic needs, followed by some common menu items.

ENGLISH-SPANISH PHRASES

English	Spanish	Pronunciation
Good day	**Buen día**	bwehn *dee*-ah
Good morning	**Buenos días**	*bweh*-nohss *dee*-ahss
How are you?	**¿Cómo está?**	*koh*-moh ehss-*tah?*
Very well	**Muy bien**	mwee byehn
Thank you	**Gracias**	*grah*-syahss
You're welcome	**De nada**	deh *nah*-dah
Good-bye	**Adiós**	ah-*dyohss*
Please	**Por favor**	pohr fah-*vohr*
Yes	**Sí**	see
No	**No**	noh
Excuse me	**Perdóneme**	pehr-*doh*-neh-meh
Give me	**Déme**	*deh*-meh
Where is . . . ?	**¿Dónde está . . . ?**	*dohn*-deh ehss-*tah?*
the station	**la estación**	lah ehss-tah-*syohn*
a hotel	**un hotel**	oon oh-*tehl*
a gas station	**una gasolinera**	*oo*-nah gah-soh-lee-*neh*-rah

English	Spanish	Pronunciation
a restaurant	**un restaurante**	oon res-tow-*rahn*-teh
the toilet	**el baño**	el *bah*-nyoh
a good doctor	**un buen médico**	oon bwehn *meh*-dee-coh
the road to . . .	**el camino a/hacia . . .**	el cah-*mee*-noh ah/*ah*-syah
To the right	**A la derecha**	ah lah deh-*reh*-chah
To the left	**A la izquierda**	ah lah ees-*kyehr*-dah
Straight ahead	**Derecho**	deh-*reh*-choh
I would like	**Quisiera**	key-*syeh*-rah
I want	**Quiero**	*kyeh*-roh
to eat	**comer**	koh-*mehr*
a room	**una habitación**	*oo*-nah ah-bee-tah-*syohn*
Do you have . . . ?	**¿Tiene usted . . . ?**	tyeh-neh oo-*sted?*
a book	**un libro**	oon *lee*-broh
a dictionary	**un diccionario**	oon deek-syow-*nah*-ryo
How much is it?	**¿Cuánto cuesta?**	*kwahn*-toh *kwehss*-tah?
When?	**¿Cuándo?**	*kwahn*-doh?
What?	**¿Qué?**	keh?
There is (Is there . . . ?)	**(¿)Hay (. . . ?)**	eye?
What is there?	**¿Qué hay?**	keh eye?
Yesterday	**Ayer**	ah-*yer*
Today	**Hoy**	oy
Tomorrow	**Mañana**	mah-*nyah*-nah
Good	**Bueno**	*bweh*-noh
Bad	**Malo**	*mah*-loh
Better (best)	**(Lo) Mejor**	(loh) meh-*hohr*
More	**Más**	mahs

English	Spanish	Pronunciation
Less	**Menos**	*meh*-nohss
No smoking	**Se prohibe fumar**	seh proh-*ee*-beh foo-*mahr*
Postcard	**Tarjeta postal**	tar-*heh*-ta pohs-*tahl*
Insect repellent	**Repelente contra insectos**	reh-peh-*lehn*-te *cohn*-trah een-*sehk*-tos

MORE USEFUL PHRASES

English	Spanish	Pronunciation
Do you speak English?	**¿Habla usted inglés?**	*ah*-blah oo-*sted* een-*glehs?*
Is there anyone here who speaks English?	**¿Hay alguien aquí que hable inglés?**	eye *ahl*-gyehn ah-*kee* keh *ah*-bleh een-*glehs?*
I speak a little Spanish.	**Hablo un poco de español.**	*ah*-bloh oon *poh*-koh deh ehss-pah-*nyohl*
I don't understand Spanish very well.	**No (lo) entiendo muy bien el español.**	noh (loh) ehn-*tyehn*-doh mwee byehn el ehss-pah-*nyohl*
The meal is good.	**Me gusta la comida.**	meh *goo*-stah lah koh-*mee*-dah
What time is it?	**¿Qué hora es?**	keh *oh*-rah ehss?
May I see your menu?	**¿Puedo ver el menú (la carta)?**	*pueh*-do vehr el meh-*noo* (lah *car*-tah)?
The check, please.	**La cuenta, por favor.**	lah *quehn*-tah pohr fa-*vorh*
What do I owe you?	**¿Cuánto le debo?**	*kwahn*-toh leh *deh*-boh?
What did you say?	**¿Mande?** (formal) **¿Cómo?** (informal)	*mahn*-deh? *koh*-moh?

English	Spanish	Pronunciation
I want (to see) . . .	**Quiero (ver) . . .**	*kyeh*-roh (vehr)
a room	**un cuarto** or **una habitación**	oon *kwar*-toh, *oo*-nah ah-bee-tah-*syohn*
for two persons	**para dos personas.**	*pah*-rah dohss pehr-*soh*-nahs
with (without) bathroom	**con (sin) baño**	kohn (seen) *bah*-nyoh
We are staying here only . . .	**Nos quedamos aquí solamente . . .**	nohs keh-*dah*-mohss ah-*kee* soh-lah-*mehn*-teh
one night.	**una noche.**	*oo*-nah *noh*-cheh
one week.	**una semana.**	*oo*-nah seh-*mah*-nah
We are leaving . . .	**Partimos (Salimos) . . .**	pahr-*tee*-mohss (sah-*lee*-mohss)
tomorrow.	**mañana.**	mah-*nya*-nah
Do you accept . . . ?	**¿Acepta usted . . . ?**	ah-*sehp*-tah oo-*sted*
traveler's checks?	**cheques de viajero?**	*cheh*-kehss deh byah-*heh*-roh?
Is there a laundromat . . . ?	**¿Hay una lavandería . . . ?**	eye *oo*-nah lah-*vahn*-deh-*ree*-ah
near here?	**cerca de aquí?**	*sehr*-kah deh ah-*kee*
Please send these clothes to the laundry.	**Hágame el favor de mandar esta ropa a la lavandería.**	*ah*-gah-meh el fah-*vohr* deh mahn-*dahr* *ehss*-tah *roh*-pah a lah lah-*vahn*-deh-*ree*-ah

NUMBERS

1 **uno** (*ooh*-noh)
2 **dos** (dohss)
3 **tres** (trehss)
4 **cuatro** (*kwah*-troh)
5 **cinco** (*seen*-koh)
6 **seis** (sayss)
7 **siete** (*syeh*-teh)
8 **ocho** (*oh*-choh)
9 **nueve** (*nweh*-beh)
10 **diez** (dyess)
11 **once** (*ohn*-seh)
12 **doce** (*doh*-seh)
13 **trece** (*treh*-seh)
14 **catorce** (kah-*tohr*-seh)
15 **quince** (*keen*-seh)
16 **dieciseis** (dyess-ee-*sayss*)
17 **diecisiete** (dyess-ee-*syeh*-teh)
18 **dieciocho** (dyess-ee-*oh*-choh)
19 **diecinueve** (dyess-ee-*nweh*-beh)
20 **veinte** (*bayn*-teh)
30 **treinta** (*trayn*-tah)
40 **cuarenta** (kwah-*ren*-tah)
50 **cincuenta** (seen-*kwen*-tah)
60 **sesenta** (seh-*sehn*-tah)
70 **setenta** (seh-*tehn*-tah)
80 **ochenta** (oh-*chehn*-tah)
90 **noventa** (noh-*behn*-tah)
100 **cien** (syehn)
200 **doscientos** (do-*syehn*-tohs)
500 **quinientos** (kee-*nyehn*-tohs)
1,000 **mil** (meel)

TRANSPORTATION TERMS

English	Spanish	Pronunciation
Airport	**Aeropuerto**	ah-eh-roh-*pwehr*-toh
Flight	**Vuelo**	*bweh*-loh
Rental car	**Arrendadora de autos**	ah-rehn-da-doh-rah deh ow-tohs
Bus	**Autobús**	ow-toh-*boos*
Bus or truck	**Camión**	ka-*myohn*
Lane	**Carril**	kah-*reel*
Nonstop	**Directo**	dee-*rehk*-toh
Baggage (claim area)	**Equipajes**	eh-kee-*pah*-hehss
Intercity	**Foraneo**	foh-rah-*neh*-oh
Luggage storage area	**Guarda equipaje**	gwar-dah eh-kee-*pah*-heh
Arrival gates	**Llegadas**	yeh-*gah*-dahss
Originates at this station	**Local**	loh-*kahl*

English	Spanish	Pronunciation
Originates elsewhere	**De paso**	deh *pah*-soh
Stops if seats available	**Para si hay lugares**	*pah*-rah see eye loo-*gah*-rehs
First class	**Primera**	pree-*meh*-rah
Second class	**Segunda**	seh-*goon*-dah
Nonstop	**Sin escala**	seen ess-*kah*-lah
Baggage claim area	**Recibo de equipajes**	reh-see-boh deh eh-kee-*pah*-hehss
Waiting room	**Sala de espera**	*sah*-lah deh ehss-*peh*-rah
Toilets	**Sanitarios**	sah-nee-*tah*-ryohss
Ticket window	**Taquilla**	tah-*kee*-yah

2 Menu Glossary

Achiote Small red seed of the *annatto* tree.

Achiote preparado A Yucatecan prepared paste made of ground *achiote,* wheat and corn flour, cumin, cinnamon, salt, onion, garlic, and oregano.

Agua fresca Fruit-flavored water, usually watermelon, cantaloupe, chia seed with lemon, hibiscus flour, rice, or ground melon-seed mixture.

Antojito Typical Mexican supper foods, usually made with *masa* or tortillas and having a filling or topping such as sausage, cheese, beans, and onions; includes such things as *tacos, tostadas, sopes,* and *garnachas.*

Atole A thick, lightly sweet, hot drink made with finely ground corn and usually flavored with vanilla, pecan, strawberry, pineapple, or chocolate.

Botana An appetizer.

Buñuelos Round, thin, deep-fried crispy fritters dipped in sugar.

Carnitas Pork deep-cooked (not fried) in lard, and then simmered and served with corn tortillas for tacos.

Ceviche Fresh raw seafood marinated in fresh lime juice and garnished with chopped tomatoes, onions, chiles, and sometimes cilantro.

Chayote A vegetable pear or mirliton, a type of spiny squash boiled and served as an accompaniment to meat dishes.

Chiles en nogada Poblano peppers stuffed with a mixture of ground pork and beef, spices, fruits, raisins, and almonds. Can be served either warm—fried in a light batter—or cold, sans the batter. Either way it is then covered in walnut-and-cream sauce.

Chiles rellenos Usually poblano peppers stuffed with cheese or spicy ground meat with raisins, rolled in a batter, and fried.

Churro Tube-shaped, breadlike fritter, dipped in sugar and sometimes filled with *cajeta* (milk-based caramel) or chocolate.

Cochinita pibil Pork wrapped in banana leaves, pit-baked in a *pibil* sauce of *achiote,* sour orange, and spices; common in the Yucatán.

Enchilada A tortilla dipped in sauce, usually filled with chicken or white cheese, and sometimes topped with *mole* (*enchiladas rojas* or *de mole*), or with tomato sauce and sour cream (*enchiladas suizas*—Swiss enchiladas), or covered in a green sauce *(enchiladas verdes),* or topped with onions, sour cream, and guacamole *(enchiladas potosinas).*

Escabeche A lightly pickled sauce used in Yucatecan chicken stew.

Frijoles refritos Pinto beans mashed and cooked with lard.

Garnachas A thickish small circle of fried *masa* with pinched sides, topped with pork or chicken, onions, and avocado, or sometimes chopped potatoes and tomatoes, typical as a *botana* in Veracruz and Yucatán.

Gorditas Thick, fried corn tortillas, slit and stuffed with choice of cheese, beans, beef, chicken, with or without lettuce, tomato, and onion garnish.

Horchata Refreshing drink made of ground rice or melon seeds, ground almonds, cinnamon, and lightly sweetened.

Huevos mexicanos Scrambled eggs with chopped onions, hot green peppers, and tomatoes.

Huitlacoche Sometimes spelled "cuitlacoche." A mushroom-flavored black fungus that appears on corn in the rainy season; considered a delicacy.

Manchamantel Translated, means "tablecloth stainer." A stew of chicken or pork with chiles, tomatoes, pineapple, bananas, and jicama.

Masa Ground corn soaked in lime; the basis for tamales, corn tortillas, and soups.

Mixiote Rabbit, lamb, or chicken cooked in a mild chile sauce (usually chile *ancho* or *pasilla*), and then wrapped like a tamal and steamed. It is generally served with tortillas for tacos, with traditional garnishes of pickled onions, hot sauce, chopped cilantro, and lime wedges.

Pan de muerto Sweet bread made around the Days of the Dead (Nov 1–2), in the form of mummies or dolls, or round with bone designs.

Pan dulce Lightly sweetened bread in many configurations, usually served at breakfast or bought in any bakery.

Papadzules Tortillas stuffed with hard-boiled eggs and seeds (pumpkin or sunflower) in a tomato sauce.

Pibil Pit-baked pork or chicken in a sauce of tomato, onion, mild red pepper, cilantro, and vinegar.

Pipián A sauce made with ground pumpkin seeds, nuts, and mild peppers.

Poc chuc Slices of pork with onion marinated in a tangy sour orange sauce and charcoal-broiled; a Yucatecan specialty.

Pozole A soup made with hominy in either chicken or pork broth.

Pulque A drink made of fermented juice of the maguey plant; best in the state of Hidalgo and around Mexico City.

Quesadilla Corn or flour tortillas stuffed with melted white cheese and lightly fried.

Queso relleno "Stuffed cheese," a mild yellow cheese stuffed with minced meat and spices; a Yucatecan specialty.

Rompope Delicious Mexican eggnog, invented in Puebla, made with eggs, vanilla, sugar, and rum.

Salsa verde An uncooked sauce using the green tomatillo and puréed with spicy or mild hot peppers, onions, garlic, and cilantro; on tables countrywide.

Sopa de flor de calabaza A soup made of chopped squash or pumpkin blossoms.

Sopa de lima A tangy soup made with chicken broth and accented with fresh lime; popular in Yucatán.

Sopa de tortilla A traditional chicken broth–based soup, seasoned with chiles, tomatoes, onion, and garlic, served with crispy fried strips of corn tortillas.

Sopa tlalpeña (or *caldo tlalpeño*) A hearty soup made with chunks of chicken, chopped carrots, zucchini, corn, onions, garlic, and cilantro.

Sopa tlaxcalteca A hearty tomato-based soup filled with cooked *nopal* cactus, cheese, cream, and avocado, with crispy tortilla strips floating on top.

Sope Pronounced "*soh*-peh." An *antojito* similar to a *garnacha,* except spread with refried beans and topped with crumbled cheese and onions.

Tacos al pastor Thin slices of flavored pork roasted on a revolving cylinder dripping with onion slices and juice of fresh pineapple slices. Served in small corn tortillas, topped with chopped onion and cilantro.

Tamal Incorrectly called a tamale (*tamal* singular, *tamales* plural). A meat or sweet filling rolled with fresh *masa,* wrapped in a corn husk or banana leaf, and steamed.

Tikin xic Also seen on menus as "tik-n-xic" and "tikik chick." Charbroiled fish brushed with *achiote* sauce.

Torta A sandwich, usually on *bolillo* bread, typically with sliced avocado, onions, tomatoes, with a choice of meat and often cheese.

Xtabentun Pronounced "shtah-behn-*toon.*" A Yucatecan liquor made of fermented honey and flavored with anise. It comes *seco* (dry) or *crema* (sweet).

Zacahuil Pork leg tamal, packed in thick *masa,* wrapped in banana leaves, and pit-baked, sometimes pot-made with tomato and *masa;* a specialty of mid- to upper Veracruz.

Index

See also Accommodations and Restaurant indexes below.

General Index

Accommodations

Restaurants